Nargis Walker, Nancy O'Brien, Hilary Whiteside
With thanks to Lorna Smith for advice and editorial input

Published by BBC Educational Publishing, BBC White City, 201 Wood Lane, London W12 7TS

First published 2001, reprinted twice

Colour reproduction, printed and bound by Sterling Press, Northamptonshire.

ISBN 0 563 54235 7

To place an order, please telephone Customer Services on 01937 541001 (Monday - Friday, 0800 - 1800) or write to BBC Educational Publishing, P.O. Box 234, Wetherby, West Yorkshire, LS23 7EU.

Visit the BBC Education website at: www.bbc.co.uk/education

Contents

Contents

Introduction

The AS Guru™ service from the BBC, covering books, television programmes and an extensive website (see more details on the page opposite), is your essential guide to study skills at AS Level. It offers you a route through the key elements of your course, from start to finish, to help build your confidence and really enjoy the subject. It starts with the fundamentals, explaining the concepts you need to know, then allows you to move on and apply your knowledge.

Who is AS Guru™ English for?

The service is intended for any student making the transition from GCSE to English at AS Level. For many students, the change is exciting – but also a bit intimidating. The demands of study can seem overwhelming and the work more difficult than you might have expected. AS Guru™ is intended to help you make this transition as smoothly and as painlessly as possible. If you intend to carry on studying for the full A Level, it will be equally useful, as it aims to help you learn the language and vocabulary of the subject you're studying.

The book, *AS Guru™ English,* is especially aimed at those students who will be studying the English Literature and English Language and Literature Syllabuses. However, it is useful to all students of English, since it's been written by specialist teachers, two of whom are principal examiners with leading exam boards.

About this book

The book is divided into five sections, which focus on Prose, Poetry, Drama, Writing and Language. This ensures that you will cover the main areas of Literature and Language that the Exam Boards require you to study.

All the skills you develop in the reading and writing sections can be applied equally to any type of text you study: prose, poems or plays.

The Language section links Language with Literature and guides you through grammatical terms, language in context and sytematic language frameworks.

At the back of this book are some useful reference pages. You'll find exemplar essays, the AS Level Assessment Objectives, the different examination board specifications and two glossaries, one of literary terms and one of language terms. Words that are in the glossaries are shown in **bold** the first time they are used on each page where they appear.

Features in this book

- Throughout the book, Guru tips appear in the margin. These are tips and reminders from the experts which will help you to learn, practise and revise.

- Specific links to the website and television programmes are pointed out in margin boxes, too. There are also markers to show where your AS Level work could help you to compile your Key Skills portfolio. See more about this on page 8.

- Quotations and examples appear in green boxes within the text, so you can pick them out instantly when you're skimming the book.

- At the end of each section there are some tasks to help you practise what you've learnt. No answers are given, as each student could reply differently, but there is guidance to help you see what would make a good answer, where appropriate.

GURU TIP
Remember to check with your teacher which exam board syllabus you're following and when and how each part of the course will be assessed.

GURU TIP
There's helpful advice in boxes like this throughout the book.

GURU TV
These boxes show a link with the AS Guru™ TV programmes.

GURU WEBSITE
Where there's a close link with the AS Guru™ website you'll see this box.

Information boxes give you extra facts and details.

Study skills

An important aspect of the shift from GCSE to AS Level is the change in type of study skills you need. This book looks at many of the skills you need to develop, and you'll find more help in the Study Skills section of the website (see the address below). The site contains help on how to prepare for exams, and how you can improve your writing, reading and understanding.

> There's also an AS Guru Study Skills video available:
> Price £9.99 Code: EDUC 7126

The full AS Guru™ service

AS Guru has been created to allow you to use books, the Intenet and television to create the most comprehensive study programme possible in English and other subjects (see details below). You can visit AS Guru™ English online at:

> http://www.bbc.co.uk/education/asguru/english

Here, you will find up-to-date information, text-specific revision material for Literature, wide-ranging examples of language in use and changing over time, sample questions and model answer plans, and examiners' comments and analysis of effective exam answers.

You will find details of when the TV programmes are being broadcast on the website and in the *Radio Times*, or other good TV listings magazines.

> **Details of other AS Guru™ subjects available now are:**
>
> **BIOLOGY**
>
> **Book:** ISBN 0 563 54241 1
> **website:** http://www.bbc.co.uk/education/asguru/biology
> **Television:** see details on the website and in the *Radio Times*, or other
>   TV listings magazines.
>
> **GENERAL STUDIES**
> **Book:** ISBN 0 563 54236 5
> **website:** http://www.bbc.co.uk/education/asguru/generalstudies
> **Television:** see details on the website and in the *Radio Times*, or other
>   TV listings magazines.
>
> **MATHS**
> **Book:** ISBN 0 563 4234 9
> **website:** http://www.bbc.co.uk/education/asguru/maths
> **Television:** there are no television programmes for Maths.

Key skills

Your work at AS Level can help you to gain a new, extra Key Skills qualification. This award shows that you've developed important life skills that you'll need after your studies; skills that are in demand by employers and Further Education establishments. There are six Key Skills, but only three of them – Communication, Information Technology and Application of Number – contribute to the Key Skills qualification. (The other three 'wider skills' are listed below, for your information.) To gain a Key Skills qualification, you need to collect a portfolio of evidence which demonstrates your level of competence in the three main Key Skill areas. There are three levels of award (1–3) and you should aim to meet the criteria laid down for level 3 (see below). Anytime you're asked to be involved in a class discussion, write an essay, make a presentation, research or carry out a project, you have opportunities for adding to your portfolio of evidence (so take a copy of your work!). You'll find several suggested ways of demonstrating your competence with Key Skills throughout this book.

C3	**Communication level 3**
C3.1a	Contribute to a group discussion about a complex subject.
C3.1b	Make a presentation about a complex subject, using at least one image to illustrate complex points.
C3.2	Read and synthesise information from two extended documents that deal with a complex subject. One of these documents should include at least one image.
C3.3	Write two different types of documents about complex subjects. One piece of writing should be an extended document and include at least one image.

IT3	**IT level 3**
IT3.1	Plan, and use different sources to search for, and select, information required for two different purposes.
IT3.2	Explore, develop, and exchange information and derive new information to meet two different purposes.
IT3.3	Present information from different sources for two different purposes and audiences. Your work must include at least one example of text, one example of an image and one example of numbers.

N3	**Application of number level 3**
N3.1	Plan, and interpret, information from two types of sources, including a large data set.
N3.2	Carry out multi-stage calculations to do with: amounts and sizes; scales and proportion; handling statistics; rearranging and using formulae. You should work with a large data set on at least one occasion.
N3.3	Interpret results of your calculations, present your findings and justify your methods. You must use at least one graph, one chart and one diagram.

The three 'wider skills' are:	
WO3	Working with others level 3
LP3	Learning performance level 3
PS3	Problem solving level 3

Prose

This section concentrates on prose. Essentially, though, the skills you'll be acquiring are skills that you will be able to transfer just as easily to poetry or drama.

Part of your exams will focus exclusively on the study of prose texts and you need to be prepared for this. At first glance, prose may seem to be the most accessible, or readable, of the three literary genres (prose, poetry and drama). For many people, poetry can seem the most difficult to approach, and drama, which you normally see performed rather than on the page (when you have to imagine what is happening as well as reading the lines) can also seem to require more effort.

What this section aims to do is to give you the confidence to move on to the other genres without feeling intimidated. You'll learn how to read and gather information from a text and then organise this information in meaningful ways. You will then be able to turn your reading into sound critical comment.

Where possible in this book, Key Skills have been highlighted for you. As this section is largely theoretical, you'll find that Key Skills have not been highlighted quite so often. However, there are suggestions of where you might be alert to acquiring some of the Key Skills in Communication. To some extent, you will have to use your own judgement as to where a piece of work would fulfil the criteria for Key Skills, such as when you are reading a complex critical work to support your essay, when you are in group discussions presenting your ideas from research, or when you are reporting to the class on an area of research.

This may all sound a little unfamiliar and worrying, but there's plenty in this book that will help and reassure you. You'll find that you already know some of the terms and have understood some of the ideas from GCSE English. You'll already be doing some of the critical tasks unconsciously without even knowing that you're doing so. You'll just be putting a name to them.

Learning to read critically will help you to enjoy books more, not less. Reading carefully, seeing the writer's craft and understanding the ways in which writers create meaning might even inspire you to become one yourself.

Being a critical reader

GURU WEBSITE
For more advice on how to read novels critically, check out the AS Guru™ website:
www.bbc.co.uk/asguru/english

As an AS Level student of English, you will probably already be reading widely both for entertainment and for information. You might wonder, therefore, why there is a whole section on reading literature in this book. After all, isn't reading a skill you already have? Well, you do, but there's more to reading texts in English than simply reading them through.

Learning how to really 'read' your text is crucial to being successful at this level. At GCSE you will have read your texts and thought about what the author or poet is trying to say. You will have looked at the ways in which the writer creates meaning and uses styles and techniques to bring the text to life. However, now what you have to do is to take this a stage further and become an altogether more 'critical' reader.

What is a critical reader?

When you hear the word 'critical' in the context of AS Level English, it's not about finding fault with the text (although it's possible that you might), but using the word in a positive sense, to understand how a writer creates meaning. Perhaps the best way to explain this is to look at the questions you might ask as readers.

You should constantly ask yourself what the writer is trying to say and what a text might mean. These are important questions as they help you make sense of, and use, what is written on the page. Critical readers, however, ask more in-depth questions than these and can use all the evidence they gather to support their responses.

Here are some of the most important questions to ask yourself when you read.

GURU TIP
A 'reading' of the text refers to how you interpret it and what meanings and messages you feel it conveys.

> **How** does the writer achieve meaning?
>
> **What** different meanings can be made of this text and is one reading more convincing than the others?
>
> **Why** does the writer present ideas in this way?
>
> **When** – what considerations of time and place could have affected the writer?

You will also need to learn and be able to use the technical language with which to discuss and argue your point of view with others. Like any other subject that you have studied, English has its own vocabulary that allows you to talk to others who 'speak the same language'. When you study English, the language you need to learn is the language of critical comment.

Learning the language of critical comment

GURU TIP
There's more about style and technique in the section on poetry.

Once you have learnt some of the terms (the words in the language), you'll find that you can discuss your ideas more easily and confidently.

The specialized language will allow you to use a single word when referring to something quite complex so that you can express your ideas succinctly and clearly. For example, you will be able to use a word such as 'closure' to explain how a problem is resolved at the ending of a story (see more about closure on page 13).

Learning this language is easier than you think. It's what you have been doing throughout your years in school and for each subject you have studied. The rest of this section of the book will help you to learn the language.

How to become a critical reader

- You need to be responsive and alert.
- You should be endlessly inquisitive and ask questions of the text.
- You must be imaginative.
- You also need to be sensitive.

These are the essential enthusiasms that you need to bring to a text and the text will repay you by feeding your enthusiasm. Critical reading is certainly not boring.

What will reading critically do for you?

- It will help to satisfy some of your curiosity about other worlds and other people and what matters to them, and it will make you hungry to find out more.
- It will colour your imagination and help you to see through other eyes even as you remain rooted in your own reality.
- It may not make you a nicer person, but it will help you understand and make sense of other people's thoughts and feelings, even if you don't agree with them.
- It will help you to understand and value the craft in writing.
- It will train you to think in a way that helps you to reason and argue your point of view persuasively, not just in this subject but in your other subjects and in social situations.
- It will help you to value your own opinions and to have confidence in what you have to say.

Not least, reading critically will help you to gather your ideas, form your opinions, argue your case and write the kind of essays that will help you to pass your exams. How you read will shape how you respond. So, although the sections on reading prose, poetry and drama, and the writing section are presented separately in this book, you will realize just how closely the reading and writing are bound together.

The rest of this section of the book will direct you towards asking the right sorts of questions and interpreting the answers in interesting and challenging ways. However, the most important thing is that you remain engaged with the text and respond in your own highly individual way. After you have consulted all the critics, listened to your teachers and your classmates, in the end, what will matter is what you think and how well you justify your reading. You become 'the critic'.

> **GURU TIP**
> In this section, you will learn about the vocabulary you need to discuss literature critically.

Being a good critic

Books are written to be enjoyed, and any study of them has to recognize this. However, good critics not only enjoy the text but bring to it their imagination and intelligence; their thoughts, emotions and experience.

For example, often, when you are reading for your own entertainment, you rush through the start of a book so that you can get to the 'real' story. You barely notice that openings offer a way into the book. Most writers know that if you don't like the start of a book, you may simply not read the rest of it. As a critical reader, you would look closely at the opening and decide how successful the writer has been in drawing you in.

If you can do this, at the start and throughout a book, then your response to the story will be informed, personal and convincing – which is just what the examiner is looking for.

What is narrative?

Narrative simply means story. People tell stories all the time; it's a major social and cultural activity. You confide your experiences to friends; you read and listen to literature. Religious beliefs, advertisements and films all contain narratives.

At AS Level you study narratives because they say something about people; they contain the ideas, values and beliefs of the societies in which they are created. Studying them can help you to understand yourself and others better.

One definition of narrative is that it is a chain of events, happening over a period of time, which is organised and presented to a reader or listener in a particular form.

When you are reading, think about this definition and ask yourself:

> **Which** events are selected?
>
> **How** are they connected and ordered?
>
> **What** has been left out and what has been emphasised?
>
> Through **whose** eyes have the events been presented?
>
> **What** does the narrative mean?

Analysing narrative

Here are some definitions and specific ideas to help you analyse a narrative and study its significance. Firstly, you need to know the difference between the terms narrative, plot and narrator.

Narrative: The sequence, or order in which events actually took place, which you can gather from the text.

Plot: The order of events in the text, which may be very different from the way the actual events took place. Reordering the events in this way allows the writer to create mystery, to put together key events which may have happened a long time apart, and to place emphasis on a key event.

The writer may use many techniques to achieve this, such as:
- different narrators
- flashbacks
- letters and diaries
- recollections by characters.

Narrator: The **narrator** *tells* the story and this can affect the way you respond to the story. Authors may use one narrator or several. Sometimes the narrator is a character in the story.

Theories of narrative

Many critics have written their own theory or ideas about narrative. It's well worth finding out about some of them because they offer ways to see things differently. Each individual tends to see things in a particular way. Your understanding of narrative can be affected by your background and experiences, the society in which you live, and even your gender.

GURU TIP

Here is a list of terms introduced in this section. Find out what they mean here and then practise using them in class or with your friends. narrative, narration, narrator, story, plot, structure, closure, ideology, selection and foregrounding.

GURU TIP

Narrative = chain of events

over a period of time

organised in a particular form

over a period of time

presented to a reader or listener.

GURU WEBSITE

Look at the AS Guru website for more on structure and theme: www.bbc.co.uk/ asguru/english

Narrative structures

Literary critics have different theories about the structure of narrative, meaning an underlying framework that can be used to describe all narratives. One critic, Tzvetan Todorov, believed that all narratives have the following underlying structure:

Equilibrium ——————→ Disruption or conflict ——————→ New equilibrium
(balance or stability)

This theory suggests that the narrative is driven by the need to resolve a conflict or problem. Once the problem has been solved, things can return to a sense of order. The nature of the problem and how it is sorted out is crucial to understanding the story's meaning or meanings.

Another theory, suggested by the critic Claude Levi Strauss, is that stories are based around 'the conflict of opposing forces'. There might be opposing characters, groups or places; or even opposing forces within the same character. The forces might be:

- Good vs. Evil
- Civilised vs. Primitive
- Strong vs. Weak
- Hero vs. Villain
- Rationality vs. Irrationality

These differences are often exaggerated in narratives to create drama and conflict. This theory sees the world in terms of 'binary oppositions', which just means two opposites, winners and losers.

Closure

How a story ends is an important part of the meaning of a narrative. Unlike stories in real life, narratives need an ending. The critical term for this is closure. The way the narrative closes (perhaps in a marriage or death, punishment or salvation, evil defeated or triumphant), carries with it a strong message, or moral, which emphasises certain values or views about what the world should be like, in other words, an ideology.

Selection, foregrounding and silences

What a writer selects to focus on in a story, how he or she re-orders the plot, leaves out or repeats details, expands or summarises certain points, can create a whole range of effects. When a writer concentrates on giving you the detail of one event (foregrounding) and tells you little or nothing about another (silence), he or she is making a deliberate selection and you should question why this is – perhaps it's for dramatic effect or perhaps it shows the writer's bias.

Using the terms

Once you feel you have understood the terms introduced in this section, try to start using them when you discuss literature. The more you use them, the more naturally they will come up in your discussions and essays. Your teacher will help you to use them correctly.

KEY SKILLS

Discussions that you have in class about different critical approaches could meet the Key Skill criteria for **C3.1a**, a **group discussion about a complex subject**. Remember to check that your evidence meets all the criteria.

Prose

GURU TIP

There is more in this book about narrators and narrative voice on pages 16-19.

GURU TIP

For more on silent voices, see the section on Reading for meaning (on page 28).

GURU TIP

The examiner will be looking to see if you can use the correct critical terms in your writing, so it's a good idea to try using them in class and in your coursework as much as possible.

Narrative openings

Looking at the opening paragraph of one of your set texts is a good way to begin your training as a critical reader. The opening lines of any piece of writing give you valuable information about what's to follow. Here, the focus is on prose writing.

Looking at a narrative opening

Opening paragraphs can contain information about some, or all, of the following:

- plot
- character
- setting
- **genre** (or the *type* of story)

At the same time, the writer will try to make sure that the reader is interested enough to want to continue reading. It's a good idea to try and extract as much information as you can from the opening of each of your set texts.

Here is the opening paragraph of a novel by David Guterson called *Snow Falling on Cedars*. The story begins in America in 1954 at the trial of a Japanese–American fisherman charged with murder. The context of the story (the time and place in which it's set) is an important factor. Less than ten years before, America was at war with Japan. During the Second World War, many Japanese–Americans were interned in camps because they were seen as a threat to the security of America.

When you first read this passage, you are immediately faced with a number of questions about the character, the type of story it is, and the issues raised by the descriptions of time, place and person.

> The accused man, Kabuo Miyamoto, sat proudly upright with a rigid grace, his palms placed softly on the defendant s table — the posture of a man who has detached himself insofar as this is possible at his own trial. Some in the gallery would later say that his stillness suggested a disdain for the proceedings; others felt certain it veiled a fear of the verdict that was to come. Whichever it was, Kabuo showed nothing — not even a flicker of the eyes. He was dressed in a white shirt worn buttoned to the throat and gray, neatly pressed trousers. His figure, especially the neck and shoulders, communicated the impression of irrefutable physical strength and of precise, even imperial bearing. Kabuo s features were smooth and angular; his hair had been cropped close to his skull in a manner that made its musculature prominent. In the face of the charge that had been leveled against him he sat with his dark eyes trained straight ahead and did not appear moved at all.
>
> from *Snow Falling on Cedars* by David Guterson

Reading the passage

Here are some suggestions for how to read the passage critically:

- **Read it through once**. You could speed read it the first time, just to get the gist.

- **Read it again**. This time, read more slowly with greater attention to detail. Start to ask yourself questions (how? what? why? when?) and form some ideas about plot, character and genre (the *type* of story). You may feel that this will be a detective story: you know that a crime has been committed and that a man is standing trial.

- **Now look closely one more time**. It's worth looking again for anything that offers an alternative reading of the character. Find out more about this on the next page.

GURU TIP
Later in this section, you'll learn more about the different aspects of narrative openings, such as genre.

GURU TIP
There is a separate section on pages 32-35 on context.

GURU TIP
It can help to annotate, or make notes, in your text (if you are allowed). You could underline words and phrases that interest you.

GURU TIP
If you look closely at the **diction** (language of a writer), it can help you to understand character, setting and ideas more clearly.

Analysing the passage

Take a closer look at characterisation in the opening passage of *Snow Falling on Cedars*. The passage focuses entirely on the character of Kabuo Miyamoto. Some questions you could ask yourself are:

> **What** is the author telling you about him?
>
> **What** are your impressions of this man?
>
> **How** does the author give you these impressions?
>
> **Why?**

You could make a list of all the words and phrases that seem to tell you something about Miyamoto: his physical appearance, his character and his behaviour. If you looked at this list of words used, what sort of picture do you have of this man?

You're told he sat '*proudly upright*', '*rigid*', '*detached*', that he showed '*nothing – not even a flicker of the eyes*'. He seems to betray no emotion, even at his own trial.

He is described as giving the impression of '*irrefutable strength*', as being '*precise*' and '*imperial*'. His features are '*smooth and angular*' and his hair is '*cropped close to his skull*' so that his '*musculature was prominent*'. Is there something almost dangerous or threatening about this man? That he appears to '*show disdain for the proceedings*', plus his '*imperial bearing*', suggest arrogance as well as detachment.

Link this with the fact that you are watching his trial and you might conclude him to be a guilty man. Is this the impression the author wants you to have?

An alternative reading

If you look closely for an alternative reading of the passage, there's one line at the start that could suggest a different interpretation: 'Some in the gallery would later say... '. There is a hint that Miyamoto's appearance and behaviour are being judged by people who are unsympathetic towards him. For example, they 'think' his stillness 'suggested disdain for the proceedings'. They don't know this, they are simply guessing. Is this character being presented through the hostile eyes of others who, for some reason, dislike him? Are you seeing him from their point of view?

More questions about the text

Some other questions you could ask are:

- Is there the beginning of a plot here?
- Where is this set and is there some significance in the setting?
- What can I discover about any other characters in this story?
- How are they presented?

Gaining deeper understanding

As you read on in this book, you will become even more aware of the context in this story. Kabuo is a Japanese–American on trial just after the Second World War. This provides a clue to the hostility of the people watching in the gallery. You might begin to ask:

- Will the story deal with issues of race and prejudice?
- How will the narrative develop?
- Is Miyamoto a guilty man?

It's these unresolved questions or 'narrative enigmas' which keep you reading.

> **GURU TIP**
> The description of Miyamoto answers the first two questions: **what** you are being told and **how** you are told it.

> **GURU TIP**
> If you feel you are being presented a character from a particular point of view, you might then want to ask **why**?

> **KEY SKILLS**
> At this point, any presentation you make as a result of a group discussion or a piece of research could meet the criteria for the Key Skill **C3.1b**, **making a presentation about a complex subject**.

Narrative voice and persona

The narrative voice, or point of view, is important in your understanding of character. In this section, you will learn how an author's choice of narrative voice affects your response to a story, a character or dilemma (problem). It's one of the most important considerations for a writer as it can determine whether or not you feel sufficiently drawn into the story to continue reading.

Defining persona

Persona means a 'mask'. In prose, poetry or drama, it's the way in which a writer chooses to address an audience.

Why does the writer use this 'mask'?

Adopting a persona gives a writer a 'filter' for certain views, a voice for ideas and opinions not necessarily his or her own.

Although the persona may take the form of a character in the book, the views of the character are not necessarily the views of the author, which may in fact be very different.

What is the effect of using this literary device?

Sometimes, there are several narrators in a text, whose viewpoints, perspectives and characters may differ quite a bit, even when they are describing the same event.

Think of it this way: imagine you were telling a story about a particular problem you are having with your parents. You would want to tell the story in such a way that your listener would feel some sympathy for you. But what if the same story was told by one of your parents? The chances are you might not even recognise it as the same story. You could say that each person presents their own version of the story. In other words, the story is biased by the viewpoint of the storyteller. It makes you wonder if any story can really be told objectively and without bias.

Examining the narrative voice

The book, *Frankenstein*, by Mary Shelley is one of the best examples of the way in which the narrative voice can affect your response to a story.

In this book, Shelley has created three different narrators whose stories are closely interwoven. The character Walton, an explorer bound for the North Pole, begins and ends the narration through a series of letters that he is writing to his sister while his ship is stranded in a sea of ice. While writing of his hopes and fears to his sister, he rescues and later befriends a stranger, Victor Frankenstein. Victor in turn tells his story, and that of the Creature which now pursues him, to Walton. This is a complex narrative of stories within stories, and each narrator has a distinctive voice.

If you were able to visualise the structure of the story, you might see it as a series of boxes within boxes. Since Walton's story provides a sort of outline for the other narratives, he could be called the frame narrator.

The first person narrative

First person narrative is when a narrator speaks directly to the reader using the word 'I'. All three of Shelley's narrators speak directly to you. The question you might ask yourself here is: Why has she chosen to write like this?

GURU TIP

Narrative voice is the voice or point of view of the person telling the story.

Persona is the character an author adopts to present a particular point of view.

GURU TIP

Here's a list of useful terms: persona, narrative voice, first person narrative, the frame narrator, the omniscient narrator, the unreliable narrator, the implied author, the intrusive author. You can find out about all of these in this section.

GURU WEBSITE/TV

For more information on narrative and **narrator**, check out the AS Guru™ TV programmes and the website : www.bbc.co.uk/asguru/english

Here are some reasons you might find:

- The first person narrator seems to be taking you into his confidence and inviting your sympathy.
- You are presented with each individual narrator's point of view.
- It makes you aware that, as in real life, the same event can be experienced by different people in different ways.
- It makes you wonder about whose story you should believe. Which, if any of them, are to be believed or are they all unreliable narrators?

The writer has carefully chosen her technique to heighten your awareness of the individual demands of each character for your sympathy. Each character speaks directly to you, and you may feel your emotions swayed first by one character, then by another. You may find it difficult to distinguish between hero and villain.

Walton's view

The narrative begins with Walton describing Victor Frankenstein as an individual with very special qualities. '*I never saw a more interesting creature,*' comments Walton on first meeting him and then adds soon after:

> I begin to love him as a brother; and his constant and deep grief fills me with sympathy and compassion. He must have been a noble creature in his better days, being even now in wreck so attractive and amiable.
>
> extracts on pages 17–19 from *Frankenstein* by Mary Shelley

Walton continues his account in these highly emotive terms, telling us that Victor Frankenstein excites his '*admiration*' and '*pity*', that he is '*noble*' and '*gentle, yet so wise; his mind is so cultivated, and when he speaks, although his words are culled with the choicest art, yet they flow with rapidity and unparalleled eloquence.*'

Victor's story

After these descriptions from a seemingly objective observer, you are prepared to believe that you are in the presence of an extraordinary, heroic individual. When later you hear Victor's story of his scientific quest to create life, to bestow 'life upon lifeless matter', you believe this is an intellectual and honourable goal. Victor, the much loved and privileged son of doting parents, feels he has a duty to mankind, and the elevated prose he uses to describe his mission, convinces us of his noble intentions. He seems a man obsessed with the desire to benefit humanity.

> No one can conceive the variety of feelings which bore me onwards, like a hurricane, in the first enthusiasm of success. Life and death appeared to me ideal bounds, which I should first break through and pour a torrent of light into our dark world. A new species would bless me as its creator and source; many happy and excellent natures would owe their being to me. No father could claim the gratitude of his child so completely as I should deserve theirs.

You may react with horror and pity for Victor when you discover that the result of these high ideals is a less-than-perfect, hideously deformed and monstrous Creature. You may feel sympathy for Victor as he makes his getaway from '*the wretch – the miserable monster*' that he has created. '*He might have spoken, but I did not hear; one hand was stretched out, seemingly to detain me, but I escaped and rushed downstairs.*' You feel that you can understand Victor's terrible disappointment at all his great plans going wrong.

Prose

GURU TIP
Pay attention when you read to the way in which a writer creates a voice. For example, Mary Shelley varies the diction (language) of each narrator. Note the formal, old-fashioned terms of address the Creature uses.

When you move on to volume two of *Frankenstein*, you will find one of the most powerful justifications for using more than one voice in a novel. Here you are introduced to the voice of the Creature who has just been described as a '*wretch*' and a '*monster*', and you hear his pitiful lament at the way he has been treated by his Creator.

The Creature speaks

After the first two terrible deaths in Victor's family, accidental rather than pre-meditated murder on the part of the Creature, the two meet on an icy wasteland, where Frankenstein, in a rage, refers to his creation as '*Devil*', '*vile insect*', '*abhorred monster*'. When you hear the Creature respond, however, you may find that, far from accepting Victor's descriptions of him, you are moved instead by the misfortune and despair of the abandoned Creature. The Creature says:

> All men hate the wretched; how, then, must I be hated, who am miserable beyond all living things! Yet you, my creator, detest and spurn me, thy creature, to whom thou art bound by ties only dissoluble by the annihilation of one of us... Do your duty towards me, and I will do mine towards you and the rest of mankind... But I will not be tempted to set myself in opposition to thee. I am thy creature, and I will be even mild and docile to my natural lord and king, if thou wilt also perform thy part, the which thou owest me. Oh Frankenstein, be not equitable to every other and trample upon me alone, to whom thy justice, and even thy clemency and affection, is most due. Remember that I am thy creature... Everywhere I see bliss, from which I alone am irrevocably excluded. I was benevolent and good; misery made me a fiend. Make me happy and I shall again be virtuous.

How do you feel about Victor now?

The 'hero' is revealed as selfish, insensitive and neglectful of his responsibilities.

Although the Creature proceeds to take the most terrible revenge, do you still sympathise with Victor?

Re-examine your reactions to Victor

Do you still feel pity for the destruction of his dreams? Or, do you feel that all the misery heaped upon him is a direct result of his desire to play God?

The evident emotional pain in the speech and the comparison you are forced to make between Victor's childhood: '*No human being could have passed a happier childhood than myself. My parents were possessed by the very spirit of kindness and indulgence,*' and his undignified and hasty abandonment of the helpless being he has created, is made only too obvious by the Creature's delivery of his side of the story.

- What remains of your original impression of Victor?

- Should you abandon your reading of him as a heroic figure?

- What of Walton's assurances of his extraordinary character?

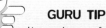

GURU TIP
It can be useful to underline or highlight significant parts of a text, such as the quotes picked out on this page. If you cannot write in your book, try jotting quotes in a notebook.

A fresh look at the text

Now have a look at an earlier portion of the text where Walton is describing why he feels that Victor might have been '*the brother of my heart*'. Here he describes how Victor has become his confidant, the only person to whom he can describe his overwhelming desire to conquer the natural elements.

> I was easily led by the sympathy he evinced, to use the language of my heart, to give utterance to the burning ardour of my soul; and to say, with all the fervour that warmed me, how gladly I would sacrifice my fortune, my existence, my every hope, to the furtherance of my enterprise. One man s life or death were but a small price to pay for the acquirement of the knowledge which I sought for the dominion I should acquire and transmit over the elemental foes of our race.

There is a chilling echo in Walton's speech of Frankenstein's obsession; of his hubris (presumptuous pride). You can sense Walton's own ambition to be god-like, with the power of life and death over others. Even Frankenstein sees this in him and it's this that leads him to tell his own story as a warning to the other man.

- How reliable is Walton's opinion of Frankenstein?
- Does he paint such a glorious picture of Victor because he sees in him a reflection of himself?
- Is he an **unreliable narrator**, whose words and motives the author forces you to question?

The book deals with a number of issues, such as:

- the boundaries of science and questing
- duty and responsibility
- innocence and justice
- humanity and inhumanity.

On a very simple level, the story tests your moral response to these issues through the use of very personal and persuasive voices that tell you their stories and beg you to understand.

Other voices

You may recognise other types of voices in this story, and in other narratives. Here are a few you might find.

The implied author

This is a narrator who is not actually a character in the story but who appears to stand back and tell you a story objectively. Using this device, the real author is able to persuade you that what you are hearing is an unbiased account of the narrative. Remember, though, that there is no such thing as an unbiased voice. The fact that the narrator is choosing to tell you some things, that is foregrounding, and maintaining a silence about other matters, means there is a purely subjective process of selection going on. In other words, you are being told only what the narrator wants you to know.

The omniscient narrator

This kind of narrator is god-like and knows the outcome of the story.

The intrusive or interfering narrator

This kind of narrator interrupts the narrative with an opinion or an explanation which reminds you that the story is not real but an artificially constructed piece of writing.

Prose

What is genre?

GURU WEBSITE
The AS Guru website has a section dedicated to major literary genres: www.bbc.co.uk/asguru/english

Genre is the way in which you can classify the literature that you read. You will probably enjoy reading books since you have chosen to do AS Level English. Even so, it's not unusual to hear students complaining that they enjoy reading books and talking about them but what is the point of classifying them, pulling them apart and discussing structure and context?

You may not have thought it, but this is something that you do all the time anyway. For example, you may discuss with a friend why you like a particular type of book, dislike a character, find a plot over-complicated or an ending unsatisfactory. Here are some examples of statements that you may recognise.

> *'I couldn't put this book down, but then I really like horror stories.'*

You are actually making a critical evaluation. What you are saying is:
- In my **opinion**, this is a well-written book, but I particularly like reading this **genre**.

> *'I found it hard to believe that anyone could be so totally nice and kind in the circumstances. He's just not believable.'*

The critical evaluation you are making here is:
- The writer has presented a wholly **unconvincing character**, so uniformly 'nice' that the **reader** cannot quite believe in him.

> *'It's hard to follow what exactly is going on. The story jumps about too much.'*

In other words:
- The **plot** is poorly **structured**.

What you need to do at AS Level, that's different from before, is to learn how to focus more closely on what you are reading. You need to acquire the vocabulary to describe your analysis more accurately and part of this is learning how to classify what you are reading.

Defining genre

GURU TIP
Remember: genre is a way of classifying. It means a kind or type.

Genre means a kind or type.

For example, here are some words which you could say are of a type.

sofa	armchair	coffee table

If you wanted to refer to them by type, you might call them 'living-room furniture'. What makes them a type is what they share in common, which is that you would place all of these items in the living-room. This helps you to separate them from another group of words such as bed, bedside table, wardrobe, which you would refer to as 'bedroom furniture'.

Words are constantly grouped as a reference point in everyday conversation. People talk about types of:

Television programmes	Newspaper articles	Films
soap	home news	thriller
documentary	foreign news	action movie
drama	sports report	film noir

Of course, it's not always quite so easy to categorise things neatly in this way.

Which genre?

Look again at the example of the living-room furniture. What would happen if you lived in a country where you didn't have a separate room for eating, sleeping or sitting with others? Categorising the furniture as you have done would be meaningless and without any value. In other words, the way you classify depends on your culture and the shared values of your community.

For the same reason, it can be difficult to categorise certain types of texts. You may remember the Summer 2000 popular television series *Big Brother*, in which ten people were isolated from the rest of the world in a house, which one of them was made to leave each week, voted out by the other house members and the audience. It was watched and commented on by a lot of people, including the media. Here are three ways in which viewers categorised it:

- Soap
- Game show
- Sociological study (which is how some members of the academic world and some journalists saw it)

These are three different generic readings. Each group of viewers applied the key features of *Big Brother* to a different type or genre, according to their experiences.

This demonstrates two important points:

- that people always read texts of all kinds (poetry, prose, drama, film, etc.) by categorising them as types or genres
- that the categorising is not a science, and can be done differently by different groups of people, depending on their experiences and cultures.

This is an important idea to grasp. It means that you might make a different set of meanings from a text than another student. <u>Both</u> readings could be equally valid, as long as you could both demonstrate, with reference to the texts, which set of rules you had applied.

Supporting your choice of category

It's important to validate your reading by reference to the text and to the rules which you applied. For example, if you were categorising *Big Brother*, these are the rules you might highlight for some of the readings:

Genre	Shared features with other programmes in this genre
Game show	A number of contestants. Contestants are progressively reduced by a series of tests. There is an eventual winner.
Soap	The programme runs as a series. You watch the progress of the same group of people. You watch their lives and loves.

Genre provides you with an easy means of understanding how to validate your reading. 'Reading' is more of an art than a science and its interpretations are flexible. This doesn't mean any interpretations will do. To be a good critic, you need to be able to justify your reading. Justifying your reading means supporting your views by saying why you hold them. As you will see later, this has implications for the way you present your views in writing.

Prose

GURU TV
Check the TV programmes for more about genres and material on quiz shows.

GURU TIP
Generic means 'relating to genre', so a generic reading is which genre you categorise something as.

GURU TIP
Classifying texts through genre helps to make meaning of texts.

GURU TIP
A text can belong to more than one genre.

Genre in literature

In Literature, **genre** has traditionally meant the three main genres of prose, poetry and drama. This book has been divided into these main areas (apart from the section on Language and the sub-section on Writing), since this is what the Exam Boards require you to study for Literature.

Looking more closely at literary genres

Genres can be subdivided into **sub-genres**. For example:

Genre	Sub-genres
Drama	tragedy, comedy
Poetry	lyric, epic, ballad
Prose	horror, fantasy, romance

Often, there are clues on the cover of a book, such as the pictures and the 'blurb' on the back, which tell you what the text is about. You may even have looked for a specific genre by using the shelf headings in a bookshop, such as travel writing, biography, science fiction. However, it is also possible to find clues in the way a book is written to predict what genre to expect.

One sub-genre in prose which is easily recognised by the writing is the detective novel. Every detective novel has similar features, such as:

- A crime, probably a murder.
- Details of a specific time and place in which the crime took place.
- A detective, sometimes a professional, often an amateur who is skilled in logical reasoning or who has a 'nose' for solving a crime.
- An opening which introduces a seemingly unsolvable mystery that puzzles the reader.
- Once solved, the solution is easily understood by the reader.
- An ending with the criminal being punished in some way.

Two well-known writers of this genre are Agatha Christie and P.D. James. If you have read any of their novels, you will recognise the list of features above. Some of these features are shared with other genres, such as 'mystery novels' and 'crime fiction' by authors such as Michael Dibdin.

Deciding which genre

Since the emphasis in this section is on prose, the four extracts on the next three pages are all examples of this genre. Read them one at a time, carefully, and before you look at the comments beneath each extract, try this process:

- Make a list of the features you recognise.
- See if you are able to decide which sub-genre each of the extracts might belong to by comparing the key features of the text with other books you have read.
- Could some of the features belong to more than one genre?

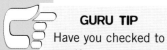

GURU TIP

Have you checked to see if you know what sub-genre some of your set texts belong to?

Extract A

Returning from the field one afternoon, towards an evening which has not yet announced itself by any noticeable diminution of the sun s brilliance, Peter Claire sees a young woman in the garden. She is gathering flowers. As the musicians come towards her, she raises her head and smiles at them, and Jens Ingermann and the other players bow to her and she nods to them and they walk on. But Peter Claire stops.

He stands by a sundial, pretending to read time from the shadow of the brass pointer, but in reality staying only that he may say a word to this person whom he has never before seen at Rosenborg. She wears a grey silk dress. Her hair is brown, neither dark nor fair. He notices that her hands are so small that she has difficulty holding the quantity of flowers she has gathered. Shall I...may I...assist you? he stammers.

Oh, she says, looking up at Peter Claire and on the instant faltering as if she is taking in the striking beauty of his face, No, there is no need.

But he goes to her side, lays down his lute, and holds out his hands so that she may give the picked flowers to him while she gathers some more. And so the flowers pass from her arms to his and he feels in their stems, where her hands have held them, something of the warmth of her.

from *Music and Silence* by Rose Tremain

Prose

You might have found that this was easy to categorise as a romance because it contains the following features:

- a handsome man
- a beautiful, hesitant woman
- an immediate attraction
- his wish to be of service to her.

Now look at the next two extracts. Both introduce the reader to a character who is about to be killed, yet deciding on a genre is less straightforward than you might think at first reading.

Extract B

Hale knew, before he had been in Brighton three hours, that they meant to murder him. With his inky fingers and his bitten nails, his manner cynical and nervous, anybody could tell he didn t belong — belong to the early summer sun, the cool Whitsun wind off the sea, the holiday crowd. They came in by train from Victoria every five minutes, rocked down Queen s Road standing on the tops of the little local trams, stepped off in bewildered multitudes into fresh and glittering air: the new silver paint sparkled on the piers, the cream houses ran away into the west like a pale Victorian water-colour; a race in miniature motors, a band playing, flower gardens in bloom below the front, an aeroplane advertising something for the health in pale vanishing clouds across the sky.

from *Brighton Rock* by Graham Greene

- In what ways is this extract different from the one that follows?
- Are the differences significant enough to put the texts into different categories, or do they have more in common with each other?

Extract C

> On the day they were going to kill him, Santiago Nasar got up at five-thirty in the morning to wait for the boat the bishop was coming on. He d dreamed he was going through a grove of timber trees where a gentle drizzle was falling, and for an instant he was happy in his dream, but when he awoke he felt completely spattered with bird shit. He was always dreaming about trees, Placida Linero, his mother, told me twenty-seven years later, recalling the details of that unpleasant Monday. The week before, he d dreamed that he was alone in a tinfoil airplane and flying through the almond trees without bumping into anything, she told me. She had a well-earned reputation as an accurate interpreter of other people s dreams, provided they were told her before eating, but she hadn t noticed any ominous augury in those two dreams of her son s, or in the other dreams of trees he d told her about on the mornings preceding his death.
>
> Nor did Santiago Nasar recognize the omen. He had slept little and poorly, without getting undressed, and he woke up with a headache and a sediment of copper stirrup on his palate, and he interpreted them as the natural havoc of the wedding revels that had gone on until after midnight. Furthermore: all the many people he ran into after leaving his house at five minutes past six until he was carved up like a pig an hour later remembered him as being a little sleepy but in a good mood, and he remarked to all of them in a casual way that it was a very beautiful day.
>
> from *Chronicle of a Death Foretold* by Gabriel Garcia Marquez

Is this a crime novel? Or a mystery? Are there any elements that you might find it hard to categorise, such as the supernatural events?

List those elements which you recognise. Then see if you are able to categorise the extracts by **genre**. It's possible that the books could be said to belong to more than one genre.

Extract D

> I was born in the city of Bombay... once upon a time. No, that won t do, there s no getting away from the date: I was born in Doctor Narlikar s Nursing Home on August 15th, 1947. And the time? The time matters, too. Well then: at night. No, it s important to be more... On the stroke of midnight, as a matter of fact. Clock-hands joined palms in respectful greeting as I came. Oh, spell it out, spell it out: at the precise instant of India s arrival at independence, I tumbled forth into the world. There were gasps. And, outside the window, fireworks and crowds. A few seconds later, my father broke his big toe; but his accident was a mere trifle when set beside what had befallen me in that benighted moment, because thanks to the occult tyrannies of those blandly saluting clocks I had been mysteriously handcuffed to history, my destinies indissolubly chained to those of my country. For the next three decades, there was to be no escape.

GURU TIP

Have you checked to see if you know what sub-genre some of your set texts belong to?

> Soothsayers had prophesied me, newspapers celebrated my arrival, politicos ratified my authenticity. I was left entirely without a say in the matter. I, Saleem Sinai, later variously called Snotnose, Stainface, Baldy, Sniffer, Buddha and even Piece-of-the-Moon, had become heavily embroiled in Fate — at the best of times a dangerous sort of involvement. And I couldn t even wipe my own nose at the time.
>
> from *Midnight's Children* by Salman Rushdie

Again, the extract seems to suggest more than one genre.

Is this an autobiography?

Or a political novel?

The first person narrative would suggest an autobiographical novel, yet there are several hints that there is more to this book than the history of an individual as he is born 'at the precise instant of India's arrival at Independence'. His destiny seems to be indissolubly chained to that of his country's destiny. This seems to indicate that the history of the narrator will perhaps run parallel to the political history of his country. There are also mysterious supernatural elements. How would you categorise this novel? Can you justify your choice?

The importance of genre

Many institutions need to categorise genres to order or market their products.

- Libraries use genre to guide readers in book choice.
- Publishers market their books in genres such as romance or crime fiction.
- Even your school or college will plan courses (such as your English Language/Literature course) around particular genres.

All these institutions have a powerful effect on what you choose to read and in promoting certain values. You will learn more about these values and meanings in the Language section of this book.

GURU TIP
Remember: genre in Literature refers to prose, poetry and drama.

What is Literature?

GURU TIP

A critical reader asks questions at every stage of reading and studying a text.

As an English Language and Literature student, you've probably been asked this question before. Maybe you have even asked it of yourself. Here are three extracts for you to read through carefully.

> Now, what I want is, Facts. Teach these boys and girls nothing but Facts. Facts alone are wanted in life. Plant nothing else, and root out everything else. You can only form the minds of reasoning animals upon Facts: nothing else will ever be of any service to them. This is the principle on which I bring up these children. Stick to Facts, sir!
>
> from *Hard Times* by Charles Dickens

> Know yourself, know the enemy. The princessa s task is to pry, open the lock on who the enemy is, and what his secret strategy is. Of all the weapons she can use to unlock his strategy, one of the keenest is the Five Whys . When an enemy says X, ask why. Whatever answer he gives, ask why again, ask (yourself or him) why that particular answer, then ask another why of that answer, and another. At the fifth why, you have information you can use in creating your own strategy. When you trace another s behaviour back to its cause, you get to the heart of the antagonist s strategy. The Five Whys let you see beyond what he wants you to see. See beyond his strategy and you won t be forced into reacting to his actions. You will act in a way that makes him respond to you. That makes the battle yours to win.
>
> from *The Princessa: Machiavelli for Women* by Harriet Rubin

> One night, right, we got hold of this push bike. We re riding along, me on the handlebars, through the estate, when we pass this house with the front door wide open. Liam only jumps off and legs it inside — comes out beaming — with a picture from off the wall! Shoves it on top of me and pedals for all we re worth. Can t see a thing — and going like the clappers, we are. All the way down Solomon Drive and out the other side. Did we have a laugh?! Like, imagine this poor old geezer — looking up to find a picture s been nicked off his wall while he was casually making a cup of tea in the next room or somethin !
>
> from Don t Look Back by Sandra Chick
> from *Factor 25: A Collection Of Steamy Summer Love Stories*
> free with a copy of *Bliss* magazine

Now ask yourself these questions:

- Which of these extracts would you classify as Literature?

- How did you decide which extracts were Literature and which were not?

- What features of language or style were important to you in reaching your decision?

- How are they different from those extracts which you wouldn't classify as Literature?

- Did knowing the names of any of the authors or publications have an effect on your judgement?
- If you decided any of the extracts were not Literature, what was the reason for it? How would you classify them instead?

You may find that this exercise is not quite as easy as it seems at first. It's very difficult to define what 'Literature' is. If you discuss this with your classmates, you will find that there would be a wide range of differing opinions. However, what you would also find is that there would be some points on which you would all agree.

GURU TIP
There is more discussion of this in the Language section which deals with audience profiling.

The concept of Literature

Asking the questions above will remind you just how complex the word 'Literature' can be. If you are asked to define objects such as 'table' or 'chair', you would find it easy to describe them accurately. But Literature is more an idea or a concept than something that has features which can help you define it.

The meaning people give to the word 'Literature', has more to do with their beliefs about what makes for 'good' or 'bad' writing. It's about what they value. Many texts could be described as examples of writing, but you will only choose to refer to some of them as Literature. Literature is writing to which you attach some value.

As you will have noted from the exercise above, people have different beliefs about what they should value. Your beliefs about what is valuable can be a result of your experiences, culture, the society you are a part of, your race and your gender. All of these can effect the way you respond to writing.

Influences and independent responses

You will almost certainly find that the people who surround you, and whose opinions you value or respect, will have influenced your ideas of what you define as Literature. Here is a list of people who might have influenced your opinions:

- parents
- friends
- schoolteachers
- critics
- lecturers
- publishers

Some of these will have influenced you more than others, especially if you feel that those people are 'specialists' or 'authorities' in this field. Even amongst the 'specialists', you are likely to find that opinions will differ on what constitutes Literature and what is 'good' Literature.

GURU TIP
Literature is a concept defined by beliefs and values.

This is what makes the study of Literature so exciting. You have as much to contribute through your own personal tastes, insights and ideas in determining the value of a particular text as a 'specialist' and this is why examiners are interested in your opinions on a text. Remember, though, you must be able to justify your reading.

Reading for meaning

GURU TIP
Always approach your task of critical reading by considering **how** the writer creates meaning and **how** the reader creates meaning.

You have already seen some of the ways in which a *writer* can create meaning. Now you can explore some of the ways in which a *reader* creates meaning.

Often when you are reading, you will find that you are encouraged by the writer to feel sympathy with one character or another. For example, you saw how effectively Shelley used the alternating voices of Victor Frankenstein, Walton and the Creature to change your understanding of the text (see pages 16-19). The narrative voice is just one of the ways meaning is created. In the extracts from *Frankenstein*, Shelley deliberately appealed to your sympathies. The author invited you to identify with one character, then another. This process of identification is one way a writer can convey meaning and a particular point of view.

You might ask how you can demonstrate an understanding of different interpretations of a text if all meaning is made subjectively. In other words, how can you show that it's possible for you to read the same text in different ways when your own reading is biased? One way of doing this is to try to see the text from a different point of view than your own.

GURU TIP
As an AS Level Language and Literature student, you will be expected to demonstrate that texts can have many meanings. You will probably discuss this in some detail in class.

Silent voices

What would happen, for example, if you read the story of *Frankenstein* without 'hearing' the male voices?

How would you feel about any of the three 'heroes' if you considered the impact on the women whose 'voices' are not heard? The women's views are only 'silences' in the text. Look at the women in the text:

- Walton leaves behind a loving sister to whom he writes letters, which may or may not reach her, in order to pursue his heroic goals.

- Victor abandons Elizabeth, his fiancée, in pursuit of his scientific studies, which eventually lead to her murder.

- the Creature takes vengeance on Victor because his decision to destroy the 'She' creature leaves him with a life of loneliness, not because of his savage destruction of the 'She' creature.

Seen from the women's point of view, these are not heroes, but selfish individuals who pursue their aims at any cost.

GURU TIP
You don't have to agree with another point of view than your own, you only have to show that it is possible to see things from another angle.

Foregrounding techniques

The 'silenced' voices allow the writer to foreground and emphasise, or privilege, some ideas while other ways of reading the text are hidden from the reader. Writers may use a variety of techniques to foreground an idea or aspect, such as:

- the choice of a structure, for example flashbacks which emphasise a particular moment in the **narrative**

- the repetition of certain elements, therefore giving these events an exaggerated importance

- the selective presentation of events, thus obscuring or concealing other elements which may change the focus of your reading.

All of these things can influence the way in which you read the text. Making meaning is a combination, therefore, of what the writer intends and the context in which you choose to read the text.

The aim of criticism

Some experts used to say that the aim of literary criticism was to judge the **value** of a text. This depended on how well it seemed to convey the author's intended meaning. In other words, a text was valuable if it expressed the author's ideas well. However, much modern literary theory rejects the idea that texts contain meanings put there by the author. Instead, many literary theorists now believe that texts are structures from which readers make subjective meanings. People can enrich their reading by challenging the texts and by 'reading against the grain'.

Reading against the grain

Reading the story of *Frankenstein* from the women's point of view, as shown on the previous page, would be reading it against the grain. Some critics refuse to read books in the way the writer seems to invite them to. Instead, they suggest that you should try to read from a completely different viewpoint, or ideology, and read against the grain of what the writer has foregrounded. An ideology means the collected values of a group of people with the same beliefs or interests. You don't need to share their ideology to understand why the views they hold will cause them to give a particular meaning to a text but, if you can understand their concerns and values, you can understand how they will interpret the writing.

It's possible to read against the grain with any literary text. Although this section concentrates on prose, the poem below illustrates the point very clearly. Read the poem, then the comments on the next two pages.

> Mark but this flea, and mark in this,
> How little that which thou deny st me is;
> It sucked me first, and now sucks thee,
> And in this flea, our two bloods mingled be;
> Thou know st that this cannot be said
> A sin, or shame, or loss of maidenhead;
> Yet this enjoys before it woo,
> And pampered swells with one blood made of two,
> And this, alas, is more than we would do.
>
> Oh stay, three lives in one flea spare,
> Where we almost, nay more than married are.
> This flea is you and I, and this
> Our marriage bed, and marriage temple is;
> Though parents grudge, and you, we re met,
> And cloistered in these living walls of jet.
> Though use make you apt to kill me,
> Let not to this, self-murder added be,
> And sacrilege, three sins in killing three.
>
> Cruel and sudden, hast thou since
> Purpled thy nail, in blood of innocence?
> In what could this flea guilty be,
> Except in that drop which it sucked from thee?
> Yet thou triumph st, and say st that thou
> Find st not thyself, nor me the weaker now;
> Tis true, then learn how false fears be:
> Just so much honour, when thou yield st to me,
> Will waste, as this flea s death took life from thee.
>
> 'The Flea' by John Donne

GURU TV
See the TV programmes for more about ways of reading a text - peace movement leader, Bruce Kent, has his own way of looking at First World War poetry.

Prose

GURU TIP
Reading against the grain can be useful when writing essays as it can produce challenging and highly individual responses.

Reading against the grain continued

About the poetry of John Donne

John Donne is considered by many readers to be one of the greatest writers of love poetry in the English language. He celebrates love in all its many forms:

- lustful,

- wistful,

- demanding,

- fleshly,

- or spiritual.

His poems of earthly love often contain images of the religious and spiritual, while his religious poetry often contains violent and defiantly sexual imagery. His poetry, by the very images he chooses to use, images that are against the grain of his subject matter, seem to invite some critics to read against the grain of the more usual interpretations of his poems.

A straightforward reading of 'The Flea'

- Read the poem (on page 29) through twice more.

In 'The Flea', the persona is that of a man who wishes to seduce his Beloved. He begins by addressing her in a teasing voice, as if patiently explaining a particularly simple lesson.

In the first stanza, he points out that the flea is sucking (the 's' would have been written as the long 'f' in a manuscript and he would have been well aware of the connotations) the blood of first one then the other of them, swelling as though with child. (It was commonly believed then that when couples had sexual relations, there was an interchange of blood). Thus, he argues, they are already '*married*'.

He suggests that this is an innocent act and that killing the innocent flea would be three times a sin.

He concludes by saying that just as she would not be weakened by the death of the flea, neither will she be weakened by loss of '*honour*' if she yields to him. In this poem, Donne uses the image of a flea on a woman's body, a common image in Renaissance poetry, and develops the idea into a humorous and witty poem of seduction.

You may find the language and the argument in the poem difficult to follow. However, once you have grasped the meaning, you might make the following points about the poem.

- This is a witty and humorous poem.

- The tone is lighthearted and flirtatious.

- It has a clever argument which subtly links religious images with the act of seduction.

- The speaking voice is immediate and dramatic and addresses the lover directly.

- The voice of the lover is confident and intelligent.

In the poem, you are encouraged to place yourself in the position of the impatient lover. The wit, humour and intelligence used to seduce the woman are seen as attractive qualities.

GURU TIP
It sometimes helps to read against the grain by repositioning what is foregrounded and concentrating on what is left out.

GURU TIP
Gender is a particularly interesting area to explore as ideas on the role of women and sexuality have changed dramatically in the last 50 or 60 years.

Reading 'The Flea' against the grain

Now read the poem again, and this time try reading it against the grain. One way you could do this is to read it from a feminist perspective. Remember, feminist criticism is concerned with:

- The gender assumptions in a text.
- How women in particular are presented in a text.
- The way in which literary texts either support or challenge patriarchy (the system by which power in a society is concentrated in the hands of men).

Examine the language and structure of Donne's poem with this in mind. Try to think like a feminist reading the poem. This time you might notice some details that you missed in your first reading. For example:

- The man's voice is the only one you hear.
- The woman's voice is suppressed, and even when she has something to say, you only know this because the man refers to it.
- His tone, which seemed initially to be playful and flirtatious, now sounds condescending as though he is talking to a child.
- Instead of seeming persuasive, his voice now seems bullying and sarcastic.
- All the power in the poem seems to lie with the man.

Why reading against the grain is useful

Learning to read against the grain is a useful critical technique and is important for several reasons.

- It shows that you have read the text closely and attentively.
- It demonstrates that you are able to see that different readers can create different meanings.
- It allows you to present your own reading as a well thought-out response.

All of these points are clearly valuable when you are writing your critical essays. The Examiner wants to know that you are aware that a text can have more than one meaning and that you have taken this into consideration when presenting your own view.

Beyond this exam-oriented view, reading against the grain is valuable for you personally, as it helps you to broaden your understanding and become less subjective in your judgements. If you are interested in critical theories, here is a list of some of the more influential contemporary theories that you might like to explore further.

- Marxist criticism
- Psychoanalytical criticism
- Modernism
- Post-modernism
- Structuralism

For books that will help you to read up on critical theories, see page 136.

For books that will help you to read up on critical theories, see page 136.

GURU TIP
Remember, you don't have to agree with a reading against the grain, but it may help you to see things differently or defend your own point of view more vigorously.

Prose

KEY SKILLS
Group discussions where you 'listen and respond sensitively to others, make clear and relevant contributions', for example, on aspects of culture and gender, could meet the **Key Skills** criteria for **C3.1a**. Remember to keep evidence.

Text in context

GURU WEBSITE/TV

There's a section on contexts on the AS Guru™ website: www.bbc.co.uk/asguru/english. Also, see the TV programmes for an example: the poet Elizabeth Barrett Browning in the context of her times.

KEY SKILLS
C3.2

If you have read through all the sections on prose in this book, you will now be closer to understanding the many ways in which meanings can be made from a text. You should be able to identify, for example, how all of the following can be relevant to the way in which you respond to a text.

- reading through **genre**

- values and beliefs

- narrative voice

- identification

- reading against the grain

- literary theories and criticisms

In your class, you will probably explore all of these in greater detail. One aspect of making meaning, on which the Exam Boards are putting more and more emphasis, is that AS Level students should be able to place a text in context. By this, they do not mean that you need to see the text only in terms of the writer's life, or in autobiographical terms. However, it is important to understand what might have affected the values and beliefs of writers and the texts that they produced.

KEY SKILLS

Discussion and research and presentation on this topic, could be used for Key Skills criteria **C3.2. Read and synthesise information from two extended documents about a complex subject**. Beware though, one of these must include at least one image.

Context

Writers produce their work in the context of their times. Understanding the framework in which a text is written (the historical, social, political, economic and cultural contexts in which the writer has worked), places the text against a particular background which may highlight and explain some of the concerns of the author and the text. If you know something of the context, you will be better able to make an informed critical comment on the text. (You can read some information on the context of William Shakespeare, for example, on page 59 – remember that you can apply all the critical skills you have learned in this section to all three literary genres: prose, poetry and drama.)

Probably the most immediate way in which you can recognise how context influences text is by looking closely at language. To the reader or audience, the historical perspective in language is the most easily noticed. On the most simple level of making meaning, you respond to a spoken or written text through the words you recognise and their syntax (word order).

Words and meaning

Clearly, words are important to writers because they are the tools with which they convey meaning to their readers. Literature is based on the endless variety and richness of words and the way they can be manipulated and used to convey meaning.

Writers choose words very carefully and their choice depends on a number of things:

- **denotation**: the exact meaning required

- **connotation**: the associations a word may contain.

- the sound of words

- length: monosyllabic or polysyllabic

- contrast or similarity

GURU TIP

You will learn more about denotation and connotation in the Language section.

Connotation is the meaning you might give to a word that is different from a dictionary definition of what the word 'means'. For example, the words 'simple' and 'simplistic' both denote (mean) something uncomplicated, but 'simple' **connotes** (suggests) being straightforward, a positive quality, while 'simplistic' suggests negative qualities of an exaggerated or excessive simplification.

At different times in history, words may have been spelled differently and have had different meanings and connotations. The meaning you make of a text will depend on your understanding of this.

GURU TIP
The words 'simple' and 'simplistic' are often confused by students using them in an essay. Be sure you use the right word.

Prose

Language in a historical context

Look at the extract below from *Sense and Sensibility* by Jane Austen. Austen was writing in the early half of the nineteenth century. Other authors, such as Charles Dickens, wrote books that dealt with wider social issues or, like the Brontë sisters, wrote passionate, dramatic novels. Unlike these other nineteenth century authors, Austen chose to write about the small communities that she knew well and the issues that concerned them. Her writing reflects this concern.

> Marianne rose the next morning with recovered spirits and happy looks. The disappointment of the evening before seemed forgotten in the expectation of what was to happen that day. They had not long finished their breakfast before Mrs Palmer s barouche stopped at the door, and in a few minutes she came laughing into the room; so delighted to see them all, that it was hard to say whether she received most pleasure from meeting her mother or the Miss Dashwoods again.
>
> So surprised at their coming to town, though it was what she had rather expected all along; so angry at their accepting her mother s invitation after having declined her own, though at the same time she would never have forgiven them if they had not come!
>
> Mr Palmer will be so happy to see you, said she; what do you think he said when he heard of your coming with Mamma? I forget what it was now, but it was something so droll! .
>
> *from Sense and Sensibility by Jane Austen*

- Are there any words you don't recognise in this passage? For example, the word '*barouche*'?
- Does the **syntax** or word order seem unusual or unfamiliar in any way? For example, '*said she*'?
- Do you find it unusual that Mrs Palmer refers to her husband as '*Mr Palmer*' rather than by using his first name?

The differences in the syntax and vocabulary make the writing seem far more formal than contemporary writing. However, it was natural for people to address each other formally in speech, even when they were close friends or husband and wife, at the time this was written, even though all of this may seem unusual to you when compared with the informal way in which you speak with your friends and family today.

GURU TIP
You will learn more about word sounds and syllables in the section on poetry and more about grammar in the section on language.

GURU TIP
It's often very important that you're aware of the historical context in which a book is set. Remember the opening paragraph of *Snow Falling on Cedars* (page 14)?

Now read the following passage from *Emma,* also by Jane Austen.

> Mr Elton is a very pretty young man, to be sure, and a very good young man, and I have great regard for him. But if you want to shew him any attention, my dear, ask him to come and dine with us some day. That will be a much better thing. I dare say Mr Knightley will be so kind as to meet him.
>
> With a great deal of pleasure, sir, at any time, said Mr Knightley, laughing: and I agree with you entirely that it will be a much better thing. Invite him to dinner, Emma, and help him to the best of the fish and chicken, but leave him to chuse his own wife. Depend upon it, a man of six or seven-and-twenty can take care of himself.
>
> from *Emma* by Jane Austen

There are a number points about how language changes that you would notice in this extract. For example:

- The word '*pretty*' would have had a much wider use. It would have had a totally different **connotation.**

- The spelling of the words '*shew*' and '*chuse*' has changed.

- The formality of speech, such as '*I dare say*', '*depend upon it*', and, '*I have great regard for him*' would appear different to the informal way in which you might talk to friends and parents.

- The **syntax** in '*a man of six or seven-and-twenty*', is different to the way in which you might have said this.

For most practised readers, these differences would present little or no problem. You would recognise, for example, that the word 'pretty' in this context did not carry the same connotations as in a more contemporary sense. The author isn't suggesting that the man is effeminate. As a practised reader, you would be using your experience of reading other texts in understanding that language changes.

In the same way, what you know or learn about the values, beliefs and conditions within a society at a particular historical moment could prove useful in understanding the literature written at that time.

GURU TV
See the TV programmes for material on Arthur Miller's *The Crucible* as a good example of writing in historical and political context.

Historical, social and political contexts

An awareness of the historical and social contexts in which literature is produced will allow you to demonstrate your ability to read the text and make judgements about whether, in your opinion, a writer might be supporting, challenging or merely reflecting the values and beliefs prevalent at the time. You could use the work of Jane Austen, once again, as an example.

Jane Austen in context

Jane Austen has often been criticised for being concerned only with the small problems of country life and courtship, while ignoring the larger political issues of the day. However, some critics argue that the behaviour of her characters does reflect her reaction to what was going on around her.

Jane Austen was born in 1775, the daughter of a clergyman, and so into a conservative, upper middle-class family. This class was made up of the landed gentry who possessed most of the wealth in an England that was still an agricultural society.

The most threatening event for them would have been the French Revolution in 1789. There was an enormous amount of fear that the revolutionary ideas would spread to England and affect the status and power of the landed gentry.

At the same time, there was a new and growing class of wealthy, powerful people being created by the Industrial Revolution, who challenged the old order. This was a time when there was political tension, a growing feminist debate about the role and treatment of women, and enormous social change.

Ways in which context can affect meaning

Here are some ways in which critics have responded to Jane Austen within the historical and political context of her times. Often, the critics take almost directly opposing views:

> Austen was aware of the political climate and confronts the issues indirectly by an increasing emphasis on maintaining law and order and emotional self-control. She was essentially conservative and strongly supported the old order.
>
> Deeper analysis shows that Austen was quietly subversive and sought to undermine the old order. Her attitudes were strongly in favour of change although she writes so subtly that, at first glance, she seems to support conservative values.
>
> Austen's heroines had to try and live their lives in circumstances that would be unimaginable to the modern woman. They had little or no direct control over where they went or who they met or married. The women in her stories who do best are those that show good sense and think rationally.
>
> Her heroines do manage to influence events by the control they exercise over their own behaviour. They are outwardly mild and obedient, yet they have a real distaste for patriarchal rule.

You can see here how the critics have looked at the context in which Austen was writing in order to support their view of what her writing was trying to say.

Using the context

It is important to notice that critics use the context to justify their reading of a work. What the Examiner will be looking for is to see how well you can apply the knowledge you have of the context of a text to support your reading of it. It allows you to demonstrate that you understand how a writer may have reacted to the events and ideas which surrounded him or her, even if they are not views that you share.

Of course, you can only suggest how things might have affected a writer in relation to the evidence you find in a text. Giving unnecessary autobiographical details, which have no relevance to the text, will gain absolutely <u>no</u> marks and are simply a waste of time and space.

Comment on the context only if it has some relevance to the text and your reading of it.

GURU TIP
Reading different critical works can help you to develop a good line of argument in your essays, and it should give you the confidence to express your own views – as long as they are supported by evidence from the text.

Prose

Practice

GURU TV

There's some interesting material on different ways of interpreting poetry in the TV programmes.

Task 1

Think of a familiar children's story such as *Cinderella*. Divide it into story, plot and narration. Readers usually sympathise with Cinderella because she is presented to us as poor but beautiful and badly treated.

Is it possible to apply the two theories that you have been given on page 13 to talk about the structure of the story? For example, are you able to map out Todorov's theory of the similarity of the underlying structure?

Equilibrium	$\rightarrow$	Conflict	$\rightarrow$	New Equilibrium
Cinderella lives in a happy family with her own mother and father. She is both beautiful and loved.		Cinderella's mother dies and her father remarries. Her stepmother and stepsisters are jealous and cruel. She is reduced to doing the worst jobs.		Cinderella gets to go to the ball, the prince falls in love with her and rejects the sisters. Cinderella marries the prince, the stepmother and stepsisters are humiliated. Cinderella and her prince live happily ever after.

Now try to use Levi Strauss' theory that stories are based around conflicts which are played out in the narrative as opposing forces?

Cinderella	vs.	stepmother / stepsisters
good	vs.	evil
beauty	vs.	plainness

* Can you think of any other opposite forces in the story?

* Who is defeated and who is victorious?

* Is there a moral presented in the method of **closure** (see page 13)?

You might create meaning here by accusing the stepmother and the stepsisters of being the forces of evil. However, you might change the emphasis of meaning and moral by asking other questions.

One of these might be: where was the father in all of this? Or, what if the story was narrated by the stepmother, and Cinderella was presented as beautiful but spoiled and resentful, rude to her stepmother and her stepsisters and every bit as snobbish as her sisters in her determination to marry a prince?

Would this change the way in which you understand the story? Finally, as a personal response, you might want to challenge some of the messages of the story:

Cinderella = beauty = goodness? Do you agree with this message?

Now see if you are able to apply these ideas to the more sophisticated narratives in one of your set texts.

Task 2

Look at the opening paragraph of one of your other texts. Read it through several times. Now ask the key questions of the text, what?, how?, why? and when? What are you being told about plot, character and setting? How, or in whose voice, is this information being presented to you?

- **What genre** of story is this?
- **How** is this story being presented to you, for example whose voice is used and what is emphasised and what is left out?
- **Why** is it being presented in this way, and what is the hook that keeps you reading?
- **When**: are there any considerations of time and place which you ought to notice and which affect the information you are being given? For example, how might the story have been different if it were set or written in a different time or place? (Think about gender, or the way the women / men are presented in this story.)
- What, if any, messages are contained in this story? What meaning does it have and could it be read differently?

Task 3

Using one of your set texts, work out from whose point of view the story is being told.

- Is there more than one narrator?
- Is it the intimate first person narrative or the more distanced third person?
- How does the narrative voice affect the meaning of the story?
- Why do you think the writer has chosen this voice over others in the story?
- Could your response to the story be altered if another voice had told the story?

Task 4

Here is an extract from *Heart of Darkness* by Joseph Conrad. The story is narrated by Marlow, an Englishman, who relates his adventures on a boat while travelling down the Congo at a time when Europe was expanding its colonial empires. Read the extract and answer the questions which follow.

> Now and then the boat from the shore gave one a momentary contact with reality. It was paddled by black fellows. You could see from afar the white of their eyeballs glistening. They shouted, sang; their bodies streamed with perspiration; they had faces like grotesque masks — these chaps; but they had bone, muscle, a wild vitality, an intense energy of movement that was as natural and true as the surf along their coast. They wanted no excuse for being there. They were a great comfort to look at.
>
> from *Heart of Darkness* by Joseph Conrad

- How are the Africans presented here?
- What characteristics are being foregrounded?
- Whose point of view do you see them from?
- What effect does this have on your perception of the Africans?
- What view do you have of the **narrator** by comparison?
- If you read against the grain, how would you do it and how would it alter your reading?

Key points about reading prose

Narrative

- Learning the language of criticism helps you to discuss the subject meaningfully.

- Narrative helps you to understand yourself and others.

- Theories about narratives can help you to understand the structure and meaning of narratives.

- A narrative may be read in many different ways depending on what the writer chooses to tell you and other factors, such as, narrative voice, context of time and place, and the experience and insights which the reader brings.

Narrative voice

- Narrative voice is the voice or voices which the writer chooses to tell a story.

- A writer adopts one or more personae (singular: persona) to tell his or her story.

- The choice of narrative voice is important as it is one way in which a writer creates meaning.

- The narrative voice connects the writer with the reader, encouraging a response from the reader.

Genre

- Genre is a way of recognising a 'type'.

- These types are organised by looking at a list of shared features.

- These features can be part of more than one genre.

- How you organise these features is influenced by the values of the society and culture in which you live.

- Genre is a means by which institutions which produce or market books are able to influence what you read.

Reading and making meanings

- Literature is hard to define. It's a subjective concept.

- Your beliefs and values shape what you define as Literature.

- Critical theories help you to read against the grain.

- Reading against the grain helps to widen your understanding of how meaning can be made.

Text in context

- Context is important in making meaning.

- The context of a text can highlight influences on a writer.

- Learning about the context in which a text was produced can help to explain the concerns of the writer and the society in which it was produced.

Poetry

What will you learn in this section?

→ You'll learn how to use criticism to explore poetry.

→ You'll investigate different devices, such as similes, metaphors and imagery.

→ You'll learn about the forms and conventions of poetry, such as rhyme, metre and structure.

You will find that there is a difference between studying poetry at GCSE and at AS Level. You will be expected to examine poetry in more depth and you'll be asked to comment confidently on the poet's choice of language. What you need to do, as a student, is:

- develop your skills, most of which are firmly in place from your work at GCSE Level
- have the confidence to form your own opinions.

Exploring context

It's very useful to be able to place your poetry texts in a social and historical context. Although this will be covered in your coursework, you can help yourself by doing your own background research. You'll find that some knowledge of the people and the period in which, or about which, poets are writing makes everything far more interesting and can give you a new perspective on the work.

Quotations

As in prose and drama, you will need to support all your ideas and opinions on poetry with appropriate quotations. You probably won't be able to quote more than a few words, because you simply won't have time. If you aren't allowed to take texts into the examination room, you'll have to learn some short, useful quotations. You'll discover which ones are the most useful from work and discussions in class, and the essays which you write.

Reading poetry

The dense nature of poetic writing often means that many ideas are packed into a few words, so you may need to read a poem more times, and more carefully, than a piece of prose, in order to understand it fully. However, you can approach a poem in exactly the same way as you approach a piece of prose. Poetry and prose share many of the same literary devices – as does drama, which you will see in the following section. That's why this section starts by taking a close look at some of these literary devices. You will know some of them already, from GCSE, but you need to be able to explore and discuss them in more detail for AS Level.

Similes

GURU WEBSITE
Find out more about how to analyse poetry by looking at the AS Guru™ website:
www.bbc.co.uk/asguru/english

One literary device you have probably come across before is **simile**. Similes are comparisons. Writers use similes to help you imagine certain images and feelings. Think about your own writing, or even just talking. If you're trying to describe something you've seen, or a feeling to a friend and it is outside their experience, you often do it by making a comparison with something they <u>do</u> recognise. Generally, similes are easy to identify in writing because they are so straightforward. When using a simile a writer simply says that something is **like**, or **as**, something else. For example:

- Tom's face was white **as** snow

- Daisy runs **like** the wind.

Sometimes the comparisons in a simile sound unrealistic: snow is not always very white and no one has seen the wind running. The key is that everyone understands the implication, or what the user means. So, one of the purposes of a simile is to create common understanding between a writer or speaker and his or her audience.

Adding depth

Similes can add depth and dimension to a piece of written work or dialogue. John Milton was a master of the simile. Look at this extract from 'Paradise Lost' in which he describes Satan.

> He above the rest
>
> In shape and gesture proudly eminent
>
> Stood <u>like</u> a tow r
>
> > extracts on this page from 'Paradise Lost' by John Milton

The strength of Satan's character is effectively conveyed using quite a simple comparison. Milton expands this technique by using extended, or epic similes. Several lines long, epic similes create whole pictures separate from the main text. Read Milton's description of Satan's supporters rallying together.

> <u>As</u> when the potent rod
>
> Of Amram s son in Egypt s evil day
>
> Waved round the coast, up called a pitchy cloud
>
> Of locusts, warping on the eastern wind,
>
> That o er the realm of impious Pharaoh hung
>
> <u>Like</u> night, and darkened all the land of Nile

GURU TIP
An **epic poem** is a long, narrative poem usually divided into books or parts. Its themes are generally religious or mythological.

Milton's work is enriched by these vivid images. In this example, he's using the familiar Bible story of the plague of locusts visiting Egypt to suggest the huge numbers and hideous nature of Satan's supporters. 'Paradise Lost' is an epic poem encompassing a vast theme, the 'Fall of Man', but Milton's use of the simile helps to describe divine events in familiar, human terms.

Similes in context

The similes that a poet uses reflect the social and historical background of the writer. For instance, nowadays you might read, 'his eyes were like lasers', or, 'she had a mind like a computer,' but these similes wouldn't have made sense to Milton's readers who wouldn't understand the comparisons since they refer to things not known at that time. During Milton's era, and in earlier writing, poets often used images from nature – a much more important source of imagery then than it is today. The fourteenth-century writer, Geoffrey Chaucer, was particularly fond of comparing people to animals. Here's how Chaucer portrays the Miller in 'The Prologue' to *The Canterbury Tales*.

> His berd <u>as</u> any sowe or fox was reed,
>
> And therto brood, <u>as</u> though it were a spade.
>
> Upon the cop right of his nose he hade
>
> A werte, and theron stood a toft of herys,
>
> Reed <u>as</u> the brustles of a sowys erys
>
> <div align="right">from <i>The Canterbury Tales</i> by Geoffrey Chaucer</div>

Although you may not be familiar with Middle English, you can identify and relate to the common images. Chaucer is not only describing the Miller's looks, but is also implying the Miller has a crafty nature by comparing him to a fox.

Why do writers and poets use similes?

With similes, you can:

- create an area of common understanding
- add richness to a text
- place work in a particular social and historical context
- add to the reader's understanding of a text
- express the **abstract** in concrete terms.

How effective are they?

It's not enough just to be able to identify similes. You will need to say how effective they are, what writers are trying to help you imagine, and whether they have succeeded. When you recognise a simile in a piece of writing, think about how effective the images are by asking yourself these questions:

- Is there a double-edged comment being made by the author through use of the simile (as in the example from Chaucer, which alluded to the appearance of an animal, but made you think of its character as well)?
- Can you imagine the total picture being offered by the writer? Has he or she successfully raised an image in your mind?
- Are you aware of your senses being stimulated? Which ones?
- What does the simile add to your understanding of the writing?

> **GURU TIP**
> **Colloquial language**
> is everyday language used in speech. But it doesn't necessarily mean swear words.

Poetry

> **GURU TIP**
> **berd** is a beard, **reed** is red, **cop** is top, **herys** are hairs, **erys** are ears, and **werte** is a wart in Middle English.

Metaphors

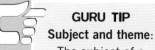

GURU TIP

Subject and theme:
The subject of a
poem is what it's
about on first
inspection.
The underlying
purpose of the poem
is the theme.

Another common literary device is the **metaphor.** A metaphor compares two things by saying that one *is* the other. The Ancient Roman author, Quintilian, explained the difference between a metaphor and a simile in this way: he adapted the simile 'he fought like a lion' into the metaphor 'he was a lion in the fight.' In other words, that person is no longer just *like* a lion, but has *become* the lion.

Extended metaphors

In the poem 'Tamer and Hawk', the contemporary poet, Thom Gunn, uses the extended metaphor of the tamer and his hawk to express his love for his partner. Look at the following extract.

> I thought I was so tough,
>
> But Gentled at your hands,
>
> Cannot be quick enough
>
> To Fly for you and show
>
> That when I go I go
>
> At your commands
>
>
> Even in flight above
>
> I am no longer free:
>
> You seeled me with your love,
>
> I am blind to other birds —
>
> The habit of your words
>
> Has hooded me
>
> from 'Tamer and Hawk' by Thom Gunn

The poet compares himself to a hawk and his lover to its tamer. As a hawk is commanded by its tamer, the poet is also commanded by his lover. Although he's not actually chained to his partner – it says he has, '*flight above*' – he's '*no longer free*' because of his love, formed through '*habit*'. His love makes him 'blind to other birds', or unwilling to pursue other relationships.

Gunn uses hawking **imagery** to sustain the metaphor, introducing words particular to hawking. For example,

GURU TIP

An **extended
metaphor** is a
metaphor which is
developed and
sustained throughout
a poem or a section
of a poem. It can
include whole books,
for example, George
Orwell's *Animal Farm*
and Lewis Carroll's
Alice in Wonderland.

- hooded

  Trained hawks wear hoods when they are not in flight.

- seeled

  Their eyes are stitched or 'seeled' as a restraint.

Think of the implication these words bring to Gunn's relationship. His love and commitment to his partner are so strong that they have blinded him to his surroundings.

You should now be able to see clearly how, through the use of metaphor, the poem is double-layered; the nature of Gunn's relationship expressed alongside the hawk and its relationship with its tamer.

Shakespeare and extended metaphor
Shakespeare effectively uses the beehive as an extended metaphor for England in *Henry V*.

> For so work the honey-bees,
>
> Creatures that by a rule in nature teach
>
> The act of order to a peopled kingdom.
>
> They have a king, and officers of sorts;
>
> Where some like magistrates correct at home;
>
> Others like merchants, venture trade abroad,
>
> Others, like soldiers, armed in their stings,
>
> Make boot upon the summer s velvet buds,
>
> Which pillage they
>
> from *Henry V* by William Shakespeare

You can break the extract down into isolated specific comparisons to see how the metaphor works:

- *Order* reigns in Henry's kingdom, like that in a beehive.
- He is king and the *honey-bees* are his subjects.
- Soldiers are *armed in their stings*.
- Bees *raid* flowers for their pollen, soldiers raid and *pillage* land.

Why are metaphors used?
Like a simile, metaphors can:

- add richness to a text
- place work in a particular social and historical context
- express the abstract in concrete terms
- add to the reader's understanding by expressing an idea in an alternative form which relates to his or her experience
- reinforce ideas by using simple and familiar images

In addition, metaphors can:

- sometimes have a stronger, bolder and more powerful effect than a simile. It is bolder to say that something *is* something else than just that it is *like* something.

Personification
This device is closely related to the metaphor. When animals, elements of nature, abstract ideas or inanimate objects are given human characteristics, this is **personification**. For example,

'The wind danced across the field, swirling round the nodding trees!'

Wind does not literally dance and trees don't nod. Dancing and nodding are human behaviour. However, personification can add a 'human' quality to a description.

GURU TIP
Metaphors add dimension to a poem by creating a variety of visual images.

Conceit and imagery

The **conceit** is related to both the **simile** and **metaphor**. It's a highly specialised literary device developed by the metaphysical poets of the sixteenth century, such as John Donne and Andrew Marvell. The metaphysical poets examined and investigated the first principles in nature and thought through their poetry. Nowadays, you might say they were going 'back to basics!'

A conceit is an over-elaborate, contrived comparison, which often seems far-fetched. A example of this is found in Donne's 'To His Mistris Going to Bed':

> O my America! my new-found-land,
>
> My kingdome, safeliest when with one man man d,
>
> My Myne of precious stones, My Emperie,
>
> How blest am I in this discovering thee!
>
> from 'To His Mistris Going to Bed' by John Donne

The poet compares his lover to America and to an Empire. Remember that this was a period of discovery and so the comparison was politically and socially topical. He further develops the idea by suggesting that his lover, like America, should be governed by one man. She is also compared to a mine of precious stones, suggesting not only beauty but material wealth. This device allows the poet to introduce a variety of diverse, often seemingly disconnected, imagery into his poetry which eventually is reconciled (or hangs together), by relating to the overall image – of an Empire, in this case.

What is imagery?

Imagery is the creation of a word picture. Its purpose is to sharpen communication with the reader by enhancing our feelings, allowing us to see, feel and hear the description. It adds another dimension to writing. An artist uses colour, tone and texture to convey his subject matter; a poet uses imagery, which includes all of the devices described in this book, and more. Visual imagery is based on colours and physical description, aural imagery on hearing – perhaps by using **onomatopoeia** or **assonance**; tactile imagery attempts to evoke strong pictures you feel you can almost touch.

Here's the opening verse to John Keats' 'The Eve of St Agnes'.

> St Agnes Eve—Ah, bitter chill it was!
>
> The owl, for all his feathers, was a-cold;
>
> The hare limp d trembling through the frozen grass,
>
> And silent was the flock in woolly fold:
>
> Numb were the Beadsman s fingers, while he told
>
>
> His rosary, and while his frosted breath,
>
> Like pious incense from a censer old,
>
> Seem d taking flight for heaven, without a death,
>
> Past the sweet Virgin s picture, while his prayer he saith.
>
> extracts on pages 44–45 from 'The Eve of St Agnes' by John Keats

GURU TIP

For more on assonance and onomatopoeia, see pages 46–47.

You get a very clear sensory picture from Keats about this particular St Agnes' Eve – you can almost feel how cold it was.

- Sheep are *silent* huddled together for warmth.
- The hare *trembles* and *limps.*
- The Beadsman's fingers are *numb.*
- It's so cold that his *frosted breath* is visible.

By using a simile to connect the incense and breath, Keats adds another sensory dimension to the picture by stimulating your sense of smell with the incense.

In the same poem, describing the feast set before Madeline and Porphyrio, Keats tempts you with:

> ...jellies soother than the creamy curd,
>
> And lucent syrops, tinct with cinnamon;
>
> Manna and dates, in argosy transferr d
>
> From Fez; and spiced dainties, every one,
>
> From silken Samarcand to cedar d Lebanon.

You can almost taste these exotic dishes.

The sounds of the words, '*jellies soother,*' and '*lucent syrops*' are more important than their literal meaning; the long, smooth sounds of the words '*soother*' and '*lucent*' make the '*jellies*' and '*syrops*' sound tempting and whet your appetite by appealing to your senses of taste and smell. The mention of the East with its rich, spicy smells adds a luxuriant quality to the image.

Keats colours in visual images for his reader. Madeline's room is cloaked in the beauty of various colours as moonlight shines through the stained glass. Look at the following extract:

> And diamonded with panes of quaint device,
>
> Innumerable of stains and splendid dyes,
>
> As are the tiger-moth s deep-damask d wings;

Specific colours aren't mentioned by Keats. Instead, you're encouraged to recall the subtle deep reds, oranges and blues of the '*tiger moth's deep damask'd wings*' – colours which share a similarity to stained glass.

The word '*diamonded*' gives shape to the colour, reminding you of leaded window panes. The elaborate image is further developed later on by using the word 'device', which relates to heraldry, reminding the reader of the medieval setting of the poem.

GURU TIP
Similes, metaphors and conceits are all forms of **imagery**.

Poetry

GURU TIP
Imagery can be divided into visual, aural and tactile.

Alliteration and other devices

GURU TIP
Alliteration
emphasises points of
interest. It can give a
poem speed and
evocative sound.

Alliteration is the deliberate repetition of a sound at the start of a group of closely positioned words. Look at the extract below.

> The men <u>shoved</u> forward, <u>shaped</u> to <u>shoot</u> at him,
>
> loosed arrows at him, hitting him often.
>
> the following three extracts from
'Sir Gawain and the Green Knight' (traditional)

In the first line, the 'sh' sound is repeated, like the 'whoosh' of arrows, and in the second line, it is the 'h' which is repeated. Medieval poetry was often told in long, oral **narratives** and alliteration was a popular device for moving the 'story' on at a fast pace.

Depending on which letter is alliterated, it can speed up or slow down a piece of writing. In the next two extracts you can hear how the repetition of the hissing letter 's' mimics speed and movement in the following:

> He <u>struck</u> the <u>steed</u> with his <u>spurs</u> and <u>sprang</u> on his way
>
> <u>So</u> forcefully...

The longer time it takes to form and say the letter 'w', and its 'woolly' sound, gives the piece a slow and gloomy feel later on as you are forced to dwell on the letter.

> It <u>would</u> have been <u>wiser</u> to <u>work</u> more <u>warily</u>.

Assonance

Assonance is simply the repetition of vowel sounds which echo through a line, or a series of lines. Wilfred Owen, in 'Anthem for Doomed Youth', refers to, 'the rifle's rapid rattle.' Here, the strong vowel 'a' is repeated in consecutive words; listen for the echo. It is particularly effective, as it mimics the 'rat-a-tat' sound of the gun firing.

Look at this extract from Lord Alfred Tennyson's narrative poem, 'Morte d'Arthur'.

> That all the <u>decks</u> were <u>dense</u> with stately forms,
>
> Black-<u>stoled</u>, black-hooded, like a dream — by <u>these</u>
>
> <u>Three</u> <u>Queens</u> with crowns of <u>gold</u> — and from them <u>rose</u>
>
> A cry that shivered to the tingling stars...
>
> from 'Morte d Arthur' by Lord Alfred Tennyson

GURU WEBSITE
There's more about
alliteration and
assonance on the
AS Guru™ website:
www.bbc.co.uk/
asguru/english

You can hear the way the short, sharp 'e' resonates in the first line in the words '*decks*' and '*dense*'. Similarly, Tennyson makes use of the rounded 'o' sound in the word '*stoled*', which he echoes through the following lines in the words '*gold*' and '*rose*'. Finally, the long 'ee' sound is repeated in the words, '*these*,' '*three*,' and '*Queens*', making you linger on them.

Remember that, in a similar way to alliteration, assonance can produce a harsh or gentle effect and you might consider what effect Tennyson was striving for in this particular passage. Often, a poet uses assonance with alliteration to produce rich, musical sounds. The technique is used continually through this poem.

Onomatopoeia

Onomatopoeia is when a word sounds like the noise it's describing. It can be used very effectively in poetry (and prose) when the author is trying to build up an impression of sound.

Wilfred Owen, in his World War I poem, 'Dulce et decorum est', describes how he could hear the blood, '*come gargling from the froth-corrupted lungs*' of a soldier who had been injured in a gas attack. The word *gargling* suggests the horrible, bubbly sound perfectly.

> wind <u>seethes</u> in the leaves around
>
> me the trees <u>exude</u> night
>
> birds night birds yell inside
>
> my ears like stabbed hearts my heart
>
> <u>stutters</u>...
>
> from 'Dulce et decorum est' by Wilfred Owen

Onomatopoeia doesn't have to be comic-book obvious. Look at this quotation from Margaret Atwood's poem, 'Half Hanged Mary'. Words such as '*seethes*', '*exudes*' and '*stutters*' are onomatopoeic; the sounds of the words suggest their meanings and are very effective in creating an atmosphere.

Enjambment

Enjambment is when there is no punctuation at the end of a line of poetry so that the sense 'runs over' into the next line. The following poem, 'Rembrandt's Late Self-Portraits', by Elizabeth Jennings, is a good example of sustained enjambment.

Notice how almost every line of this first verse deliberately flows into the following line. Think about the fluidity this lends, not only to the structure of the poem, but also how it is used to enhance the poet's meaning.

> You are confronted with yourself. Each year
>
> The pouches fill, the skin is uglier.
>
> You give it all unflinchingly. You stare
>
> Into yourself, beyond. Your brush s care
>
> Runs with self-knowledge. Here
>
> 'Rembrandt's Late Self-Portraits' by Elizabeth Jennings

Consonance

Consonance is the repetition of similar sounding consonants. In this line from Wilfred Owen's poem, 'Happiness', there is a repetition of 'l' sounds: 'No nestling place is left in bluebell bloom'.

Sibilance

Sibilance is the repetition of 's' sounds. In the poem 'Exposure', Owen describes men under attack from enemy gunfire: 'Sudden successive flights of bullets streak the silence.'

Poetry

Rhythm and rhyme

The rhythms of everyday speech can go largely unnoticed because they are so familiar but, if you listen closely to conversations, the rhythms will become apparent. You will hear stresses on certain syllables. Listening to young children can help because their speech is more unguarded and the rhythms are often more obvious. Writers sometimes attempt to reproduce these rhythms of speech. Although it's more apparent in poetry, it's not restricted to this **genre.**

Metre

Rhythm is the 'beat' of a poem and is created through the use of **metre.** The metre of a poem is the number of stressed (indicated with a /) and unstressed (indicated with a ∪) syllables in a line.

Look at these two lines from the sonnet, 'Composed upon Westminster Bridge' by William Wordsworth (see more about sonnets on page 52).

> This city now doth, like a garment, wear
>
> The beauty of the morning: silent bare

Read aloud, it's easy to hear where the stressed and unstressed syllables occur and identify a regular rhythmic pattern. In this example, there are five pairs of syllables. Each of these pairs is called a foot or metre. This type of metre is called **iambic pentameter.**

Iambic pentameter
Iambic pentameter was the most commonly-used type of metre until the twentieth century. 'Iamb' identifies the type of foot (∪/), and 'pentameter', the number of feet in the line (*pent* means five in Greek).

An iamb is an unstressed syllable followed by a stressed syllable (∪/). The word *Macbeth* is a good example. If you say it aloud, the *beth* part is emphasised more than the *Mac* part.

Five iambs in a row make an iambic pentameter. They have an unintrusive rhythm that's used to imitate the rhythm of everyday, English speech and which makes the lines flow in a natural way.

Spondee
The rhythm in a foot can vary, though to very different effect. A foot with two equally stressed syllables (//) is called a spondee. It tends to give a slow, dreary, melancholy feel to a line, for example, 'green grass'.

Anapaest
On the other hand, the two, light, unstressed syllables of the anapaest (∪∪/), as in the word 'amputee', for instance, lend pace and movement, speeding the words on.

The effect of rhythm
You do need to be able to break down lines of poetry into syllables in order to identify rhythms. Look at the section of Grace Nichols' poem, 'Alone', shown on the next page. It's really rhythmic and song-like. How does she achieve this effect?

GURU TIP
A **syllable** is a unit of pronunciation. Remember how you tapped these out on your desk?
Rabbit: two syllables.
Idiosyncratic: six syllables.

GURU TIP
There's more information about metre and rhythm in the glossary, but the only term you have to commit to memory is **iambic pentameter.**

GURU TIP
Make sure you spell the word **rhythm** correctly.

> The fat black woman
>
> sits alone
>
> gathering
>
> gathering
>
> into herself
>
> onto herself
>
> soft stone
>
> woman moan
>
> the fat black woman
>
> sits alone...
>
> from 'Alone' by Grace Nichols

Poetry

GURU TIP
Rhythm and rhyme set the pace of a poem, help the poet to convey moods, emphasise certain points, and provide a pleasing aural experience.

Read the poem out loud to yourself, noting where the stressed and unstressed beats occur. Can you identify a pattern? Does she change rhythm? Is the rhythm effective? These are some of the questions you should ask yourself when you look at a poem.

Rhythms can influence a reader's perception of a poem, so they are deliberately chosen by the poet. For example, you can see from the Wordsworth example how iambic pentameter helps a poem to glide and gives a lightness to its tone.

GURU TIP
Remember, there's no point in commenting on the rhythm if you don't explain how it adds to the mood of the poem.

Rhyme

You may expect poems to **rhyme**, and many do, especially pre-twentieth century poems. You'll certainly be familiar with rhyme in song lyrics, but poems don't *have* to rhyme. Rhyme is easy to identify, but you must be able to explain the reasons for the poet's use of rhyme, and its effects. Look at the way Grace Nichols intersperses the rhyming words '*stone*' '*moan*' and '*alone*', making the rhymes seem almost accidental. They add to the poem's song-like quality and increase your understanding of the loneliness of the central character, by emphasising these significant words.

GURU TIP
Lyrical rhyme has a song-like quality because it was originally intended to be sung. Lyrical poetry often expresses personal feelings.

Look out for rhyme in prose and in the media, especially advertising, ('For mash get Smash!'), as rhyming words stick in the memory. Poets use them for this reason too. Rhyme links words, making listening easy, and can emphasise important points, too.

Internal rhyme quickens the pace of a poem. You can hear it in this extract from Samuel Taylor Coleridge's 'The Ancient Mariner':

> The fair breeze <u>blew</u>, the white foam <u>flew</u>
>
> The furrow followed free:
>
> We were the <u>first</u> that ever <u>burst</u>
>
> Into that silent sea.
>
> from 'The Ancient Mariner' by Samuel Taylor Coleridge

Rhyming **couplets** are often used by poets to emphasise an important point. Look at the finality of the rhyming couplet at the end of Shakespeare's *Romeo and Juliet*:

> For never was a story of more woe
>
> Than this of Juliet and her Romeo.
>
> from *Romeo and Juliet* by William Shakespeare

GURU TIP
A rhyming couplet is where two consecutive lines rhyme. It can stand alone or be part of a sequence. Remember to spell **couplet** correctly.

Shakespearean **sonnets** tend to end with rhyming couplets as well. The couplet offers a thematic conclusion, or resolution, to ideas explored in the preceding lines.

Poetic form

The form of a poem is both its shape on the page and its structure. A poem's visual form allows the reader to distinguish it from other types of literature. Poets deliberately choose a particular form as this often has a bearing on the content of the poem. For instance, the traditional **sonnet** form (see page 52) might still be chosen by a twentieth-century poet who wants to write a poem about love. The formality of the sonnet form lends a sincerity to the message.

On the other hand, it would be inappropriate to write about a serious issue in limerick form because the comedy of a forced rhyming scheme can take over despite the message. In the past, tradition often governed the form of poetry but, nowadays, poets are less bound by these conventions; they adapt forms to suit their personal style and freely explore and experiment.

Verse

Poems are mostly divided into groups of lines called verses, or **stanzas**. It's this formulation that generally distinguishes poetry from prose. Verses can have a regular pattern with rhyme, metre and a specific number of lines, like sonnets. But, an irregular verse will not follow a particular pattern, and is a feature of modern poetry.

Blank verse

You could refer to this as unrhymed iambic pentameter (see page 48). The lines are unrhymed, ten syllables long (although they can have an eleventh, unstressed syllable, which doesn't 'count'), have alternating stresses and are divided into five feet. Many of the finest poems written in the English language have been written in this form and it was certainly the most popular until the turn of this century.

Elizabethan dramatists, notably Shakespeare and Marlowe, used it, and it was also prevalent in narrative poetry. Milton uses it in 'Paradise Lost', and Wordsworth in 'The Prelude'. It's a very flexible medium and, as explained on page 48, is capable of imitating normal, English speech patterns. These examples of **blank verse** are taken from *Macbeth*:

> Macbeth says,
>
> So foul and fair a day I have not seen.
>
> This is a perfectly regular iambic pentameter. The following speech by Banquo, when he first sees the wiches, shows the slightly irregular form:
>
> By each at once her choppy finger laying
>
> Upon her skinny lips: you should be women,
>
> And yet your beards forbid me to interpret
>
> That you are so.
>
> from *Macbeth* by William Shakespeare

If you want to mention iambic feet or blank verse in your exam, remember it's only worthwhile if you explain why their use is significant and what they add to the atmosphere of the scene.

Free verse

This refers to poems that do not have lines of regular or equal length. There is no planned metre and there is rarely any rhyme. The poet creates his or her own form.

Lawrence Ferlinghetti is a master of **free verse** and this example is taken from his poem 'Short Story on a Painting of Gustav Klimt'.

> They are kneeling upright on a flowered bed
>
>   He
>
>   has just caught her there
>
>   and holds her still
>
> Her gown
>
>   has slipped down
>
>   off her shoulder...
>
>   from 'Short Story on a Painting of Gustav Klimt' by Lawrence Ferlinghetti

Ferlinghetti has cleverly used the form of his poem to enhance his meaning. The cascading words act as a literal, visual representation of the gown falling off the woman's shoulder.

Quatrains

A quatrain is a poem with a stanza (or verse) of four lines. It can have any rhyme or metre. Ballads are a good example of this.

> There was a king and a glorious king.
> A king of noble fame.
> And he had daughters only one,
> Lady Diamond was her name.
>
> He had a boy, a kitchen boy.
> A boy a muckle scorn.
> She loved him long, she loved him aye,
> Till the grass o ergrew the corn.
>
>   Traditional ballad

The repetitive rhyming, rhymthic patterns of this form make it particularly appropriate to song and to being committed to memory – useful if you happen to be a medieval wandering minstrel!

GURU TIP:
Diction is the literary term given to the choice of language and range of vocabulary. See the prose section for more on diction, page 12.

Poetry

The sonnet

GURU TIP
Stanza is another
word for a verse.

GURU TIP
Remember that the
rhyme scheme of a
poem is shown by
calling the first
rhyming word a, and
any words that rhyme
with it a, as well. The
next rhyming word
that doesn't rhyme
with a is called b, as
are all the rhyming
words that match b,
and so on, using as
many letters as you
need.

Sonnets are lyrical poems, often devoted to the subject of love. The two most popular types are:

- Petrarchan: 14 lines of iambic pentameter. It's made up of two parts, the octet (first eight lines) and the sestet (final six lines). The mood or tone of the poem changes at this break. A question posed in the octet may be answered in the sestet, for example. The octet rhymes **abbaabba** and the sestet generally rhymes **cdecde**.

- Shakespearean: 14 lines of iambic pentameter, rhyming **ababcdcd efefgg** and using the octet and sestet division. The major difference is that the final couplet usually makes a statement.

Read the following poem.

> Be slowly lifted up, thou long black arm,
>
> Great gun towering towards heaven, about to curse;
>
> Sway steep against them, and for years rehearse
>
> Huge imprecations like a blasting charm!
>
> Reach at that Arrogance which needs thy harm,
>
> And beat it down before its sins grow worse.
>
> Spend our resentment, cannon, — yea, disburse
>
> Our gold in shapes of flame, our breaths in storm.
>
>
> Yet, for men s sakes whom thy vast malison
>
> Must wither innocent of enmity,
>
> Be not withdrawn, dark arm, thy spoilure done,
>
> Safe to the bosom of our prosperity.
>
> But when they spell be cast complete and whole,
>
> May God curse thee, and cut thee from our soul!
>
> 'On Seeing a Piece of our Heavy Artillery Brought into Action'
> by Wilfred Owen

GURU TIP
Voice is the point of
view of the person
narrating the poem.
See the prose section
for more about voice,
pages 16-19.

In this case, Owen's use of the sonnet form is ironic. He's retained the structure of a sonnet, but the conventional theme of love has been replaced by ideas of war and attack. Traditionally, the central character of a sonnet is the poet's mistress but, in this poem, the human love interest has been replaced by a gun – a weapon of destruction.

Alternatively, Rupert Brooke uses the sonnet form in 'The Soldier' more conventionally to express his love for his country. England is personified as a woman. Brooke uses this image as his central focus of celebration, with natural imagery, to convey his unquestioning love. Read the poem on the following page. Note that he does adapt the sonnet form in the sestet: there is no final couplet.

If I should die, think only this of me;

That there s some corner of a foreign field

That is for ever England. There shall be

In that rich earth dust concealed;

A dust whom England bore, shaped, made aware,

Gave, once, her flowers to love, her ways to roam,

A body of England s, breathing English air,

Washed by the rivers, blest by the suns of home.

And think, this heart, all evil shed away,

A pulse in the eternal mind, no less

Gives somewhere back the thoughts by England given;

Her sights and sound; dreams happy as her day;

And laughter, learnt of friends; and gentleness,

In hearts at peace, under an English heaven.

'The Soldier' by Rupert Brooke

Take a look at 'Sonnet 130' by Shakespeare, 'My mistress' eyes are nothing like the sun', shown below. Instead of the highly stylised imagery commonly used in Elizabethan poetry, Shakespeare describes his mistress in the most ordinary terms. Perhaps Shakespeare gives this ironic twist to his poem in reaction to the **hyperbole** of most Elizabethan love sonnets.

GURU TIP
Hyperbole is exaggerated language not meant to be taken literally.

My mistress eyes are nothing like the sun;

Coral is far more red than her lips red;

If snow is white, why then her breasts are dun;

If hairs be wires, black wires grow on her head.

I have seen roses damasked, red and white,

But no such roses see I in her cheeks;

And in some perfumes is there more delight

Than in the breath that from my mistress reeks.

I love to hear her speak; yet well I know

That music hath a far more pleasing sound:

I grant I never saw a goddess go;

My mistress, when she walks, treads on the ground.

And yet, by heaven, I think my love as rare

As any she belied with false compare.

'Sonnet 130' by William Shakespeare

AS Guru™ English

53

Practice

Task 1

Have a look at Simon Armitage's poem 'Very Simply Topping Up the Brake Fluid'.

Yes, love, that s why the warning light comes on. Don t
panic. Fetch some universal brake fluid
and a five-eighths screwdriver from your tool kit
then prop the bonnet open. Go on, it won t

eat you. Now, without slicing through the fan belt
try and slide the sharp end of the screwdriver
under the lid and push the spade connector
through its bed, go on, that s it. Now you re all right

to unscrew, no, clockwise, you see it s Russian
love, back to front, that s it. You see, it s empty.
Now, gently with your hand and I mean gently,
try and create a bit of space by pushing

the float-chamber sideways so there s room to pour,
gently does it, that s it. Try not to spill it, it s
corrosive: rusts, you know, and fill it till it s
level with the notch on the clutch reservoir.

Lovely. There s some Swarfega in the office
if you want a wash and some soft roll above
the cistern for, you know. Oh don t mind him, love,
he doesn t bite. Come here and sit down Prince. Prince!

Now where s that bloody alternator? Managed?
Oh any time, love. I ll not charge you for that
because it s nothing of a job. If you want
us again we re in the book. Tell your husband.

'Very Simply Topping Up the Brake Fluid' by Simon Armitage

Examining a poem in detail

Ask yourself the following questions, then look at the guidance below for help:

1. What **poetic devices** does Armitage use?
2. What is its **subject**?
3. What is the **theme**?
4. What is the **tone**?
5. Whose is the **voice**?
6. What is interesting about the **diction**?
7. How does the poet use **punctuation** for effect?
8. What about the **form**?

Guidance

1. You should be able to identify some of these from reading pages 40–47.

2. On the surface, it's about a garage mechanic guiding a woman through repairing her car, but is it really about something else?

3. Is there a gender issue? The man is patronising the woman since he doesn't think she can repair the car. Is there a generation gap? Find evidence for these ideas.

4. Distinguish between the tone implied through the man in the poem and the poet's tone. The poet has adopted the persona of the garage mechanic whose tone is sarcastic, patronising, demeaning and yet this is not the poet's view. The mechanic, when he does not have his work to hide behind, becomes less sure of himself. Some evidence for this is in the fifth verse.

5. The voice is the garage mechanic's, and yet the poet's voice does emerge. Readers are left in no doubt as to where Simon Armitage's sympathies lie.

6. The poem is a monologue. The mechanic is conducting a one-sided, biased, conversation with no response from the woman. He uses technical language. Is he trying to impress the woman? Do you think that this will impress her?

7. Several short sentences are used. What effect does this have on the movement of the poem? It moves quickly, suggesting that the woman can't respond to the mechanic's comments because he's continually speaking. The poet uses **enjambment** (see page 47) at the end of the first three verses to the same effect. He aims to mimic fast, uninterrupted conversation.

8. There are four lines to every verse, and some rhyme. Look at the endings of the second and third lines of each verse. Even when there is not an actual rhyme ('above' and 'love'), the words seem to fit together: 'screwdriver' and 'connector.'

Preparing to answer

Plenty of practice exploring poetry is the best way to build up your confidence. Having a plan and approaching questions in a methodical way will help you be prepared. Here are some things you can do before and during the exam:

- Try to memorise a list of items to look for in a poem.

- Read and make sure you understand the question.

- Write out a list of points you want to cover that will answer the question.

- Read over the poem. Re-read it and annotate points. Tick off the points as you cover them.

- Make sure that you can support your ideas with quotations from the poem. If you know what poem you'll be looking at, you could learn some useful quotations.

Key points about poetry

Poetic devices

- Similes are comparisons that use 'like' or 'as'. They help you to imagine certain images or feelings.

- Metaphors compare two things by saying that one 'is' the other. They express an idea in an alternative form which relates to your experience.

- A conceit is an over-elaborate, contrived comparison which often seems far-fetched.

- Imagery is a word picture.

- Alliteration, assonance, consonance and sibilance can all influence the pace of a poem and draw attention to sounds for a particular effect.

- Alliteration is the deliberate repetition of a sound at the start of a group of closely positioned words.

- Assonance is the repetition of vowel sounds, consonance is the repetition of similar sounding consonants, and sibilance is the repetition of 's' sounds.

- Onomatopoeia is when a word sounds like the noise it's describing. It's very effective at creating an atmosphere and highlighting specific sounds.

- Enjambment is the lack of punctuation at the end of a line of poetry so that the sense 'runs over' into the next line.

Forms and conventions

- Rhythm is the 'beat' of a poem. It helps to provide a framework for the writing and to establish a mood.

- Rhyme is when the sound at the end of one word matches the sound at the end of a nearby word. It links certain words making them memorable.

- Metre is the number of stressed and unstressed syllables in a line.

- Iambic pentameter is used to imitate the rhythm of everday speech.

- Groups of lines in a poem are verses or stanzas.

- Blank verse is unrhymed iambic pentameter.

- Free verse is poetry which doesn't have lines of regular or equal length.

- Quatrains are poems with stanzas of four lines.

- Sonnets are lyrical poems written in Petrarchan or Shakespearean iambic pentameter.

Drama

What will you learn in this section?

→ You'll learn how historical and social contexts influence playwriting.

→ You'll find out about some of the elements of drama, such as setting, lighting and stage directions.

→ You'll think about audience awareness.

→ You'll learn about dramatic devices, such as dramatic irony, soliloquies and manipulating time.

In this section, you'll be looking specifically at drama. Its history and development are covered briefly and you'll be given advice on how to study a play. You will have studied both a Shakespeare play and a twentieth-century play for your GCSE course and they may have been part of your coursework. AS Level requires you to build upon the knowledge you've gained at GCSE and to sharpen your critical skills. Remember to apply knowledge learnt in other sections of this book to your drama work.

Dramatic conventions

There's a wide variety of drama texts to study at AS Level. It's likely that you'll be studying a pre-twentieth century text and some modern drama. It's also compulsory to study Shakespeare. Whichever plays you study, the same set of rules will apply when it comes to analysing their content and structure.

You'll need to know about the dramatic conventions which have influenced drama. This section will take a general look at these conventions so you'll be able to apply the knowledge you learn here to any play you happen to be studying.

The audience perspective

Traditionally, the focus in drama has been on reading rather than viewing the play. However, study is now centred on the spectacle itself. Examination Boards require students to look at drama from an audience's perspective. You also need to be able to place the drama you are studying in some sort of social, political and historical context. Background knowledge makes studying a play much more interesting; it will make a play come alive and will give you a greater insight into the issues involved in it.

Ideally, you should try to visit the theatre yourself – to see any play, not just one you're studying. You will then become a participant and will be able to judge what it's like from the audience perspective from personal experience.

What is drama?

Drama is a form of literature, like prose and poetry. However, drama is made up entirely of speech. The speech can be composed of both poetry and prose. Think of the Shakespeare texts which you studied for GCSE. These would almost certainly have contained some poetry, probably in the form of **blank verse** (see page 50), and certainly some prose, in the form of dialogue.

In drama, you cannot learn about a character from a writer's description. You need to decide what characters are like from:

- what they say
- what they do
- what other characters reveal.

The idea of performance

The key difference between drama, and poetry and prose, is that drama is meant to be performed by actors in a theatre, or within a theatrical setting. A piece of prose or a poem *can* be read out or 'performed,' but this isn't essential to its presentation. Like all forms of literature, drama is open to interpretation from the audience or readership. But, in the case of drama, it's also interpreted by the performers and director and, perhaps, even the dramatist – if he or she is consulted. Drama is both an aural and visual experience, requiring an audience. Poetry and prose may evoke aural and visual experiences, but they are contained within the mind of the reader. They tend to be individual experiences rather than shared.

Drama through the ages

It's useful to be able to see at a glance how the drama which is performed today has emerged from the past. All dramatists are governed, either consciously or sub-consciously, by the set of 'rules' established in Ancient Greece over 2000 years ago for the writing and production of drama. Some of these 'rules' or codes of practice are discussed further within this section. The time-line below should help you to identify where the plays you're studying fit into the overall picture. You'll need to find further information to fill in the details of your particular period.

Why study Shakespeare?

During your AS English Literature course you will study one of Shakespeare's plays and you will study a further play at A2. Shakespeare is the only named author that you must study – so it's worth getting to grips with how to study his plays.

No doubt people study Shakespeare just because he's well known, but the reasons for studying him are really the ones on the following page, which have caused him to be so famous, rather than the fact that he is famous.

GURU WEBSITE/TV
For further information about Shakespeare and his plays, check out the AS Guru™ TV programmes and the website:
www.bbc.co.uk/asguru/english

Timeline showing evolution of dramatic form	Greek 4th c. BC	Mystery plays AD 11thC.	Morality plays AD 15th / 16thC.
	Aristotle set out the theories which shaped comedy and tragedy.	In England, Mystery Plays, telling Bible stories, were performed by the guilds in pageants in Coventry, York, Wakefield and Chester.	These were allegories showing the vices and virtues of man, the most famous being Everyman. They were popular until the 16th century.

- He tells people so much about human nature in general. This is probably one of the major reasons why Shakespeare's plays are still watched and studied. If the things he wrote about weren't the perennial aspects of human nature, people wouldn't be interested in watching the plays any more.

- He reveals a great deal to individuals about their own nature, too – not just about humanity in general, the point made above. Because watchers recognise so much about themselves and understand themselves better from watching or reading Shakespeare, people go on doing so through the ages.

- He's a brilliant dramatist. Shakespeare might have lots of profound things to say, but we wouldn't watch the plays unless they worked as drama. The experience of watching the plays is entertaining and spectacular as well as revealing many things about life to us.

- He's a great poet. The plays are full of memorable passages of poetry, which contribute to the enduring success of his plays.

Shakespeare briefly

William Shakespeare is probably the best-known writer in the English language, but very little is known about him as a man. This is tantalising, as it is natural to be curious about such a great writer. Here is what's known about his life.

He was born in Stratford upon Avon in 1564 and was educated at Stratford Grammar School. There, he followed the traditional curriculum of the period which placed emphasis on the study of Greek and Latin. After leaving school, it's possible that he worked in his father's leather goods shop. In 1582 he married Ann Hathaway and they had three children, Susanna, and twins, Hamnet and Judith. Shakespeare had a Protestant upbringing and, like most other Elizabethan people, he attended church on a regular basis. Ann and William spent most of their marriage apart because Shakespeare's life revolved around the London theatres.

Nothing is known of his life between 1585 and 1592 and these are referred to as 'The Lost Years,' but it is probable that he was living in London working as an actor and playwright. As his prestige grew, Shakespeare became involved with the Royal Court and was patronised by Queen Elizabeth I until the end of her reign. Shakespeare was involved in all aspects of the theatre. He made large financial investments in several London theatres. His accumulated wealth was invested in land and property around Stratford where his family remained.

Shakespeare's plays were immensely popular in his own time. Altogether, he wrote 38 plays, and 154 sonnets. During his lifetime, his plays were performed from 1592 to 1612; the first was probably *The Comedy of Errors* and the last was probably *The Tempest*. Shakespeare retired to Stratford and died on his birthday in 1616. He is buried in the parish church of All Saints in front of the altar.

In the year 1623, all of his plays were compiled in the First Folio where they were categorised into Tragedies, Comedies and Histories.

GURU TIP
Think about ways in which the play you study has social and political implications for today.

GURU TIP
Remember that you can apply much of what you've learned in the section on poetry to Shakespeare's drama.

GURU TV
There's more about Shakespeare and his historical context in the TV programmes.

Drama

Elizabethan AD 16thC.	Jacobean AD 17thC.	Restoration AD Late 17thC.	Decline AD 18thC.
Elizabeth I, 1558—1603. Prolific time for drama — Shakespeare, Marlowe, Johnson and Webster. First theatre 1576.	James I 1603—1625. Plays of cruelty, murder and revenge by e.g. Webster, Tourneur.	Charles II 1660—1685. Oliver Cromwell had closed theatres. Now came comic plays, with intrigue, the immoral rake figure and bawdy innuendo.	A decline in interest in drama until Sheridan,. Goldsmith at end of 18th century.

Playwrights and their influences

You will need to build on what you learnt at GCSE, and be able to support any statements you make in an essay with a sound argument. This means that you'll need more information. A source of further information is to look at playwrights' work in the context of the times in which they wrote and how this might have influenced them.

Like poetry and prose, drama reflects the social and historical setting in which it was written. Reading a brief social history of the period you are studying will give you a much better understanding of a play's content, and even its characters. Social and historical awareness will help you to 'read' some of the implications and double meanings which are dependent on knowing the era. For example, Shakespeare was accused of using *Richard II* to attack the reign of Elizabeth I. Critics believed that the audience was invited to compare the character of Richard II to that of Elizabeth. Since Richard II is portrayed as weak and having favourites who were damaging to his political judgement, a comparison with Elizabeth was not very favourable.

Shakespeare's England

The Elizabethan period (1558–1603) was a prolific period for drama. In fact, the first purpose-built theatre was built in 1576. Famous playwrights included Christopher Marlowe, Ben Jonson and, of course, Shakespeare. But what was Shakespeare's England like, and how might it have influenced the plays he wrote?

A harsh and violent life

Shakespeare's England certainly had no shortage of violence and miserable deaths. There was plague, and illnesses caused by poor diet and hygiene were common. People's life expectancy was short. Only a generation earlier, people had been executed for their religious beliefs during the reign of Bloody Mary. England was also under the threat of war for most of Elizabeth's reign. Do you think the violence in some of Shakespeare's plays was a reflection of the time in which they were written? Or perhaps the violence was simply a clever crowd-puller?

- Think about Shakespeare's use of violence in his historical plays. The plight of English kings was a bloody one and Shakespeare did not shy away from portraying the violence on stage. Richard II was murdered on stage and Richard III in the wings. In his tragedies, Desdemona in *Othello* met with a sticky end and Gloucester in *King Lear* was blinded on stage. Think also about Macbeth's murder of Duncan and Banquo, or the final scene of *Hamlet* in which all the main characters slaughter one another.

The influence of the Renaissance

Across Europe an exciting renaissance (rebirth) was happening in Literature, science, music and art. There was a revival of interest in the classical world and voyages of discovery introduced new cultures and ideas into the country. The merchant class grew as trade expanded and London's population increased rapidly.

- Hamlet and Laertes are portrayed as like 'new men' of the Renaissance period. They study abroad in Wittenberg – a trend amongst scholars of the time. The medieval king, Henry V, is glorified as a kind of Renaissance king, perhaps mirroring the successes of Henry VIII, Elizabeth's father, at home and abroad.

KEY SKILLS

Finding out more about Shakespeare's use of violence for a group discussion could be used to illustrate **Key Skills C3.1a 'Contribute to a group discussion about a complex subject'.** Remember to keep evidence of your research and arguments.

KEY SKILLS
C3.1a

GURU TIP

Look at the beehive extract from *Henry V* on page 43 as a metaphor for the structuring of Elizabethan society.

Superstition

Despite the Renaissance, many Elizabethans had not shrugged off medieval superstition. They put faith in astrology and many of them believed in witches, fairies and ghosts. These feature heavily in Shalkespeare's plays.

- In *Macbeth*, Shakespeare wrote in the extra scene where Hecate appears to please the monarch, James I, who had an avid interest in witches. Fairies are the protagonists in *A Midsummer Night's Dream*. Hamlet's father, Julius Caesar, and Banquo all appear as ghosts. Many Elizabethan people believed in retribution for wrong-doing. Shakespeare often addressed the ancient theme of good and evil inherited from Greek drama. Think about Macbeth and Brutus grappling with evil. Both openly debate their murderous actions and both are punished.

The divine right of kings

Most Elizabethans believed that God elected their monarch and the monarch had absolute authority – to offend the king was to offend God. They also accepted the social structure which had evolved from Medieval times, whereby the king was head of state, followed by the churchmen and nobles, the merchants and then the rest!

- Overthrowing the 'divine order' could have some serious consequences. Think about what happens in *Hamlet* when his father is murdered and the throne taken by his uncle; or to Macbeth who usurps the rightful King Duncan. On the other hand, Henry V is the epitome of good kingship, successful at home and abroad. Shakespeare did have to be careful what he wrote about the monarchy. There were factions within England who did not accept the Tudors as rightful heirs to the English throne. Arguably, Shakespeare shows support for the Tudors and Elizabeth I by depicting Richard III (a Lancastrian) as 'a lump of foul deformity'.

Influences on twentieth century playwrights

The twentieth century play which you study for AS Level will almost certainly raise some of the issues listed below and you should make sure that you read up on the social and historical background in which your play is set. Most drama texts contain useful background information, or you can use the Internet or CD ROMs. You'll find most of the playwrights you study will have their own website.

Some dramatists are influenced by specific events, such as the British playwright R. C. Sherriff, who wrote *Journey's End* in protest at the First World War. The American playwright, Arthur Miller, wrote *The Crucible* in response to the McCarthy 'witch hunts' against supposed communists in America.

Other popular twentieth century themes include disharmony within relationships, the repetitive nature of people's lives, marriage and how it stifles the individual, and the search for romance, love and excitement. Britain's Alan Ayckbourn explores many of these issues in *The Norman Conquests* as does Norwegian-born Henrik Ibsen in *A Doll's House*. Arnold Wesker, in his British 'kitchen sink' dramas, explores everyday issues which affect the 'ordinary man': marriage, employment and the changing role of women. Arthur Miller is also much influenced by the plight of the individual man in a pluralist society and the failure of the 'American Dream'. This theme is central to his play *Death of a Salesman*. Caryl Churchill, a British woman playwright, explores feminism and the role of women in *Top Girls*.

Plays can be highly politically-charged. For instance, John Osborne vents his outrage at society for its lack of political direction and its social failings in *Look Back in Anger*, introducing the 'angry young man'.

> Here are just a few of the most popular British playwrights of the 20th Century: George Bernard Shaw, Noël Coward, John Osborne, Tom Stoppard, Arnold Wesker, Terence Rattigan, Harold Pinter.

Drama

> Here are just a few of the most popular American and European playwrights of the last century: Tennessee Williams, Arthur Miller, Eugene O'Neill, August Strindberg, Henrik Ibsen, Bertolt Brecht.

> **KEY SKILLS**
> If you do in-depth research on the Internet, CD ROMs and other media, it could satisfy the criteria for **Key Skills IT3.1, 'Plan and use different sources to search for, and select, information required for two different purposes.'** Remember to record all the sources and how you used them.

Staging a play: the basic elements

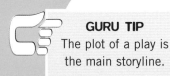

GURU TIP

The plot of a play is the main storyline.

In order to think about the audience reaction to drama, you need to consider what the play would be like as a theatrical experience. To do this, you need to think about how the play might look and sound on stage. Here are some of the elements of putting on a play that will influence its effect on the audience.

The plot

The **plot** of a play is the story, or the pattern of events which runs through the play. The traditional plot of a play can be divided into four areas:

- Opening – introduces the characters and sets the scene
- Conflict – usually the largest portion of the play, sees tension and suspense developing between the characters, leading to the climax
- Climax – a significant incident or turning point
- Resolution – the resolving, or working out, of the issues raised in the conflict and the climax

Let's look at *Hamlet* under these categories.

GURU TIP

Remember:

Opening

Conflict

Climax

Resolution

Opening: Introduction of main characters. Hamlet's meeting with the ghost of his father.

Conflict: Hamlet's delay in killing Claudius.

Climax: When Hamlet meets his father's ghost for the second time.

Resolution: The death of Claudius followed by Hamlet's and Laertes' deaths.

Do the plays you are studying fit into this traditional plot structure? Identify where conflict occurs, which major event constitutes the climax of the play and what resolutions are put forward by the playwright. The resolution does not have to be happy, witness Hamlet, but it must demonstrate a realistic conclusion to the conflict which has gone before and convince and satisfy the audience.

Sub-plots

Plays often have more than one plot. Playwrights use one, or several sub-plots to add depth and interest to their work, allowing for the development of more characters and additional story lines. Often the themes of the main plot of the play are echoed in a sub-plot. In *Hamlet*, there are several sub-plots, including the relationship between Ophelia and Hamlet, the Rosencrantz and Guildenstern episode, or Laertes' relationship with Polonius. Think how each one of these sub-plots echoes issues raised in the main plot: love, loyalty, deception and father-son relationships.

Setting

You might be asked to think about staging a play. Below are some ideas to consider when doing this. The setting includes scenery and props and any other elements of the appearance of the stage. Settings may be very elaborate or very simple, but remember that you need to have reasons for choosing the setting you do. A detailed, realistic setting of a scene is not always the most effective one.

Certain plays lend themselves to a stark set with few props. Plays have been produced using absolutely no props or set at all.

You may decide that the stark, cold feeling of Macbeth's castle is best represented by an empty stage, but, in this case, you would probably need to consider other elements, such as lighting and costume, very carefully in order to create the atmosphere you are seeking.

Some playwrights are explicit about the set they envisage and leave little to the imagination. For *A Doll's House*, Henrik Ibsen deliberately sets out to create a middle class environment on stage for his middle-class audiences. Here's an extract of a set description from the play:

> 'near the window, a round table with armchairs and a small sofa... between these doors stands a piano.'

GURU TIP
In your studies at AS Level, you won't be expected to be so detailed in your instructions, but you will need to make your intentions and the desired effect clear.

Lighting

Lighting is very important in creating atmosphere. The lighting may be straightforward – a scene that takes place in daylight in a living room wouldn't require unusual lighting. However, think about *Macbeth* which is set in a gloomy castle and includes scenes at night. How would you use light here? It can't be too dark because the audience will not be able to see, but you will not want to ruin the atmosphere by over-lighting.

Make sure that any symbolism connected with light is made obvious to the audience. In *Macbeth*, for example, darkness surrounds Macbeth in his castle, the only light comes from torches. This is intended to symbolise evil. In contrast, Macduff marches in daylight, symbolising hope. Duncan, who is wrongfully murdered by Macbeth, arrives at the castle surrounded by light.

In *Journey's End*, R. C. Sherriff uses candles to symbolise both hope and life. Candles are referred to and used as props throughout the play and are eventually extinguished in conjunction with the deaths of the soldiers.

GURU TIP
Do colours have different connotations? Are certain colours eerier than others? What about creating contrasts of light and shadow?

Costume

Costume contributes a great deal to the overall 'feel' of the play and its visual impact on the audience. Costume can anchor a play to a particular period. On the other hand, costume can be used to make an ironic statement. There has been a recent trend of setting plays by Shakespeare in a twentieth century context. For instance, the politically-charged *Richard III* has been reproduced as a 1930s' stylised military dictatorship – complete with jackboots.

Costumes may be used to give the audience clues about a character's nature. In *A Streetcar Named Desire*, Blanche almost always wears white but, at a crucial point, she appears in a red satin robe. The colours reflect the two sides of Blanche's character. Conventionally, white represents purity and innocence, while red suggests vibrancy and sexuality. In the same play, the poker players wear 'coloured shirts, solid blues, a purple, a red and white check, a light green and they are men at the peak of their manhood as coarse and direct and powerful as the primary colours.' Here, Tennessee Williams explains that the uncompromising sexuality of these men is expressed through the use of strong, primary colours.

GURU TIP
Think about Baz Luhrmann's Romeo and Juliet, starring Leonardo Di Caprio, and how he dressed his characters in costume relevant to the modern setting of Venice Beach, California.

Music

Music, too, can be used creatively in plays to set the scene and influence the mood. It may be used within the story (for a dance, or if a character sings); between scenes to indicate a change of time or place; to make your spine tingle in supernatural, scary or suspenseful scenes; for comic effect, and in lots more ways.

Drama

Stage directions

Stage directions are messages from the playwright to the actor or director, which move characters on, off and around the stage. They're also used in devising the set. The amount of detail about stage directions will depend largely on the period in which the play was written. Earlier plays may contain only simple instructions about such things as entrances and exits. However, dramatists writing now tend to be very specific in their instruction, leaving less space for individual interpretation. They see this as a way of retaining a measure of control over their work. In contrast, earlier playwrights were content to leave interpretation to the producer of the play, perhaps because they didn't consider it to be part of their writing role.

Stage directions in Shakespeare's era

If you look at the stage directions given by Elizabethan playwrights, such as Shakespeare and Marlowe, they are limited. For example, *Antony and Cleopatra* opens with the instruction, 'Alexandria. A room in Cleopatra's palace.' *Hamlet* begins with, 'Enter Barnardo and Francisco, two sentinels,' and Marlowe's *Faustus* with 'Faustus in his study.'

Stage directions in the twentieth century

In contrast, twentieth century playwrights, such as Tennessee Williams and Arthur Miller, give elaborate instructions. In fact, Tennessee Williams has been accused of writing for reading, not performing, because of the attention to detail he demands. Look at the opening to *A Streetcar Named Desire*.

> The exterior of a two storey house, corner building on a street in New Orleans, which is named Elysian Fields and runs between the L & N tracks and the river. The section is poor, but unlike corresponding sections in other American cities, it has a raffish charm. The houses are mostly white frame, weathered grey, with rickety outside stairs and galleries and quaintly ornamented gables to the entrances of both. It is first dark of an evening in early May. The sky that shows around the dim white building is a peculiarly tender blue, almost turquoise, which invests the scene with a kind of lyricism and gracefully attenuates the atmosphere of decay. You can almost feel the warm breath of the brown river beyond the river warehouses with their faint redolence of bananas and coffee. A corresponding air is evoked by the music of Negro entertainers at a bar room around the corner. In this part of New Orleans you are practically always just around the corner, or a few doors down the street, from a tinny piano being played with the infatuated fluency of brown fingers. This blue piano expresses the spirit of the life which goes on here.
>
> Two women, one white and one colored, are taking the air on the steps of the building. The white woman is Eunice, who occupies the upstairs flat; the colored woman a neighbour, for New Orleans is a cosmopolitan city where there is a relatively easy intermingling of races in the old part of town. Above the music of the blue piano the voices of people on the street can be heard overlapping.
>
> from *A Streetcar Named Desire* by Tennessee Williams

Stage directions in *A Streetcar named Desire*

The passage on the previous page is full of directions, some impossible to reconstruct and much more in keeping with the style of a novelist setting the scene at the beginning of a book. For example, Williams begins his directions with a reference to Elysian Fields (a place in classical mythology where the favoured dwell in an afterlife). The irony of this name is obvious to anyone reading all the directions because you quickly learn that the action takes place in a rough city area. However, would an audience necessarily pick up on the irony when Blanche refers to the place name later in the first scene? Similarly, 'A piano played with the fluency of brown fingers,' 'the 'redolence of bananas and coffee' and the 'lyricism of gracefulness' of the area are all very evocative to the reader, but how would you recreate these on stage?

Williams is equally uncompromising in his instructions to the actors. Blanche must sit 'in a chair very stiffly with her shoulders slightly hunched and her legs pressed close together and her hands tightly clutching her purse as if she were quite cold.' Would an actor feel some of her creativity being eroded when given such specific guidelines?

Realistically, is it possible for the playwright to transmit his perceived ideas through stage directions?

This is an interesting area for discussion.

Analysing stage directions

When looking at stage directions, you could break them down into different components. For example, with this particular play you could look at the use of music. You would need to go through the play and identify each reference to music; the blue piano, the polka tune, the raucous crescendos of the piano, etc. Then, you could ask yourself, what is the mood Williams is trying to create through the music? Of course, you would need to consider events on stage at the same time.

Alternatively, look at these stage directions from Act 2 of Ibsen's *A Doll's House*.

> *The same room. In the corner by the piano the Christmas tree stands, stripped and dishevelled, its candles burned to their sockets. Nora's outdoor clothes lie on the sofa. She is alone in the room, walking restlessly to and fro. At length she stops by the sofa and picks up her coat.*
>
> from *A Doll's House* by Henrik Ibsen

In this example, the stage directions are used to reinforce events which have taken place on stage. The Christmas tree, which was previously used to symbolise family harmony and peace, has become 'stripped and dishevelled' and acts as a visual reminder that this family has been destroyed. The agitation of Nora, the play's central character, is suggested through her relentness physical pacing on stage.

KEY SKILLS

If you take part in a group discussion, it could satisfy the criteria for **Key Skills C3.1a, 'Contribute to a group discussion about a complex subject.'** Remember to keep notes as evidence.

Drama

KEY SKILLS

If you research a topic to present in class, it could satisfy the criteria for **Key Skills C3.1b, 'Make a presentation about a complex subject, using at least one image to illustrate complex points.'** Remember to keep notes as evidence.

Dramatic devices

Dramatic devices are the conventions playwrights use to improve the effectiveness, clarity and enjoyment of a play. Many of these conventions were established in the Ancient Greek theatre and have been developed since. Certain dramatic devices go in and out of fashion. For example, Greek playwrights often used a chorus to explain or judge particular actions or characters, but you will see few twentieth century plays with a chorus.

The following section looks at some dramatic devices and examines how playwrights use them. You will be able to identify many of these devices in the plays which you are currently studying. The important question you need to ask yourself is: why is the playwright using this particular device and is it effective?

Time

Plays are acted in the present; they are in real time. Real time is the actual time during which a process takes place or an event occurs. When you watch a play, characters' actions are immediate as the plot develops through its various stages to the final resolution. Sometimes, however, a playwright wants to tell the audience about events in the past which are relevant to what's happening on stage in the present. Those events from the past might be crucial to the plot.

How can a playwright give you information about the past when a play is being acted in the present?

GURU TIP
Here are some of the dramatic devices a playwright uses to control time: chorus, soliloquy, lighting, acts and scenes, flashbacks, and asides.

- The audience can be informed of past events through a focused speech or chorus. There is an example of this, taken from *Henry V*, on page 67. Arthur Miller also uses a chorus in *View from the Bridge*: Alfieri fills the audience in on details about the main characters:

> There was no snow, but it was cold, his wife was out shopping. Marco was still at work. The boy had not been hired that day.
>
> from *View from the Bridge* by Arthur Miller

These are points which are relevant to the climax of the play.

GURU TIP
You'll learn more about soliloquy later on in this section.

- In *Richard III*, the play opens with another dramatic device, the soliloquy, through which Richard informs the audience of past events outside the realm of the play which will have a bearing on the present.

- In *An Inspector Calls*, J. B. Priestley uses the Inspector's cross-examination of the characters to raise events in the past which have a bearing on the present action on stage. Each character is guilty; each has had a part to play in the death of Eva Smith, and each is made to face his or her past actions. For example, the audience hears that, because Sheila unfairly complains about Eva's rudeness when she is trying on a coat, Eva is given the sack and becomes destitute. This plays a part in her suicide, as do the pasts of all the other characters' in the play.

- Alan Ayckbourn's trilogy, *The Norman Conquests*, is laterally constructed. In other words, each part of the trilogy shows, respectively, simultaneous events in the dining room, living room and garden of the same house during one weekend. Although each play can stand alone, the three plays interconnect and it is our insight into all three plays which gives complete understanding about the actions of the characters.

- Arthur Miller, in *Death of a Salesman*, uses flashbacks which are incorporated into the present action of the play. His main protagonist, Willy Loman, returns to the past, taking present characters with him. They become their younger selves and this action is used to inform the audience of events in the past which have relevance to Willy's present.

There are, of course, other techniques for manipulating time on stage. By dividing a play into Acts and scenes, days, weeks and months can pass in a realistic manner (time changes between scenes are usually made clear in the play programme). Set changes and lighting can also move the play quickly from one time and place to another. Asides (speech that the audience hears, but other characters don't) from characters in the play are used in much the same way as a chorus.

The chorus

The chorus was developed as a dramatic device by the Ancient Greeks. Originally, the chorus comprised a group of people who spoke in unison and commented upon action in the play. On occasions, the chorus became involved in action on stage, but this was rare, and its impartiality and detachment enabled a close relationship with the audience. The chorus reminded the audience of events which might have a bearing on the plot. Its speeches were highly stylised, often rhetorical and rhymed.

Look how Shakespeare makes effective use of the chorus in *Henry V*.

> Now entertain conjecture of a time
>
> When creeping murmur and the pouring dark
>
> Fills the wide vessel of the universe.
>
> From camp to camp through the foul womb of night
>
> The hum of either army stilly sounds,
>
> That the fixed sentinels almost receive
>
> The secret whispers of each other s watch.
>
> Fire answers fire, and through their paly flames
>
> Each battle sees the other s umbered face;
>
> Steed threatens steed, in high and boastful neighs
>
> Piercing the night s dull ear;
>
> With busy hammers closing rivets up,
>
> Give dreadful note of preparation,
>
> The Country cocks do crow, the clocks do toll,
>
> And the third hour of drowsy morning name.
>
> from *Henry V* by William Shakespeare

In this play, Shakespeare uses the chorus to open each Act and to conclude the play. This section is taken from Act 4 where he uses the chorus to describe the night preceding the battle of Agincourt. The speech contains details Shakespeare could not have reconstructed on stage. The sounds of battle preparation are heard, the whispers of the soldiers as they sit around their fires, the neighing of horses and the ring of hammers on armour create various cameo pictures of activity in the camp. The detailed description of the men's shadowed faces elicits sympathy from the audience and you feel the soldiers' fear.

GURU TIP
Chorus: a narrator or narrators who comment on the action but are not characters themselves.

Dramatic devices continued

GURU TIP
Dramatic irony establishes a double version of events on stage. It gives the audience a privileged perspective on what's happening.

Dramatic **irony** is when a character is unaware of events or circumstances of which the audience has full knowledge. A character may fail to recognise a flaw in his or her own character, which the audience can identify as their probable 'engine of destruction' (the flaw that will cause a downfall).

An excellent example of dramatic irony is in *Hamlet* where Hamlet himself meets with the Gravediggers or Clowns. Hamlet has returned to Denmark, unaware that the grave is being dug for Ophelia, the woman he has loved and rejected. Hamlet has no knowledge of the consequence of his actions in rejecting her and accidentally killing her father, Polonius, but the audience is well aware.

Hamlet:	What man dost thou dig it for?
First clown:	For no man, sir.
Hamlet:	What woman, then?
First clown:	For none, neither.
Hamlet:	Who is to be buried in t?
First clown:	One that was a woman, sir; but, rest her soul, she s dead.

extracts on pages 68–69 from *Hamlet* by William Shakespeare

As you read or watch this scene, the tension builds as you wait for the moment when Hamlet finds out that it's Ophelia who's to be buried.

Soliloquy

GURU TIP
Remember that Shakespeare was very fond of using soliloquies in his plays and that they are very useful for telling you what's going on in the mind of the character.

A **soliloquy** is when a character on stage utters his thoughts aloud, sharing them with the audience. It was a popular device with Elizabethan and Jacobean dramatists.

There are many advantages to the soliloquy:

- it creates a relationship between the speaker and the audience
- it allows for self-revelation on the part of the character
- it can be used to refer to events off stage
- it can be used to refer to significant events outside the immediate realm of the play.

Look at Hamlet's first soliloquy:

> O that this too too solid flesh would melt,
>
> Thaw and resolve itself into a dew,
>
> Or that the Everlasting had not fix d
>
> His canon gainst self-slaughter. O God! God!
>
> How weary, stale, flat, and unprofitable
>
> Seem to me all the uses of this world!
>
> Fie on t! ah fie! tis an unweeded garden
>
> That grows to seed; things rank and gross in nature

Possess it merely. That it should come to this!

Possess it merely. That it should come to this!

But two months dead: nay, not so much, not two:

So excellent a king; that was, to this,

Hyperion to a satyr; so loving to my mother

That he might not beteem the winds of heaven

Visit her face too roughly. Heaven and earth!

Must I remember? Why, she would hang on him,

As if increase of appetite had grown

But what it fed on; and yet, within a month —

Let me not think on t — Frailty, thy name is woman!

A little month, or ere those shoes were old

With which she follow d my poor father s body,

Like Niobe, all tears — why she, even she —

O God! a beast, that wants discourse of reason,

Would have mourn d longer — married with my uncle,

My father s brother — but no more like my father

Than I to Hercules: within a month:

Ere yet the salt of most unrighteous tears

Had left the flushing in her galled eyes,

She married. O most wicked speed, to post

With such dexterity to incestuous sheets!

It is not, nor it cannot come to good:

But break, my heart, for I must hold my tongue.

GURU TIP
Hamlet's soliloquy gives the audience a deep insight into his character and engages their sympathy.

Drama

What can the audience learn about Hamlet's character, his thoughts and his feelings from this? Here are some ideas.

- He is deeply unhappy and angry.
- He loved his father and is grief-stricken.
- He believes women are weak.
- He is disgusted by his mother's hasty marriage to his uncle, Claudius.
- He sees the marriage of his mother and his uncle as immoral.
- He believes his father was a better man than Claudius.

How might an audience react to this speech?

- They would sympathise with Hamlet's plight.
- They would recognise Hamlet's dignity, intellect and sensitivity.
- They would feel uneasy about events.
- It would influence their reactions to Claudius and Gertrude.
- They might even be able to anticipate some of the plot.

Conventional genres in drama

The Ancient Greeks divided their plays into two categories or genres, Tragedy and Comedy, and this division was still in evidence up until the Restoration (see the time line on pages 58-59). Remember how Shakespeare's plays are divided into Tragedies and Comedies? The themes of seventeenth and eighteenth century drama moved towards an interest in more mundane situations, which inevitably involved more down-to-earth characters, whose everyday language did not lend itself to the elevated themes of true tragedies. It was this change also that put an end to tragedy in the classical sense. Newly-evolved characters lacked the charisma and magnificence of the tragic hero and were not involved in the complex issues raised by playwrights, such as Shakespeare and Marlowe, who wrote of kings and their concerns. Themes tackling social problems and personal inadequacy replaced the classical ideas of good and evil. There has been fierce debate as to whether it is possible for twentieth century plays to contain a tragic hero. One possible candidate put forward is that of Willy Loman in Arthur Miller's *Death of a Salesman*. You will have to decide for yourself!

What you will need to know as an AS Level student are some of the rules which govern the structure of a tragedy. You also need to understand the meaning of the phrase tragic hero.

What is tragedy?

The word originates from the Ancient Greek word 'tragoidia', meaning goat song, which seems rather obscure, but possibly originates from Greek dramatists receiving a goat as a prize for writing a good play. Its origins lie in Ancient Greece where the rules for writing a tragedy were crafted by Aristotle in his *Poetics*.

A tragedy is drama which has a serious theme and generally ends in one or more of the principal characters suffering or dying. Look at *Macbeth* in this context. *Macbeth* certainly has a serious theme. One of its themes is about how ambition can change a good person into an evil one. *Hamlet,* too, fits into the category of a tragedy. For a start, most of the main characters die during the course of the play! Hamlet suffers because of his inability to act in revenge of his father's death, the woman he loves dies, his friend Polonius turns against him and this is just the start of the list.

Often, an audience will have much sympathy for a tragic hero – why, you might ask yourself? For example, it's possible to admire Macbeth's defiance and his refusal to dilute his purpose, despite the fact that he has committed regicide and several other murders on his route to the throne. Similarly, it is easy to sympathise with Hamlet, he is an endearing character who has been wronged.

What you also need to understand and memorise are the following terms. They are the original Ancient Greek set of 'musts' to appear in a tragedy.

Hamartia

This means a tragic flaw. Every tragic hero should be highly-regarded, but should be less than perfect. This imperfection is identified as Hamartia. Think of the flaws exhibited by Shakespeare's tragic heroes:

- Othello's jealousy
- King Lear's arrogance
- Macbeth's ambition
- Hamlet's inability to take action
- Coriolanus's pride and arrogance

KEY SKILLS C3.1a/C3.1b

GURU TIP

A tragic hero is a play's central focus. He is governed by fate and possesses character flaws which contribute to his downfall.

KEY SKILLS

If you research a complex topic, either for a group discussion, or to present to others, it could satisfy the criteria for **Key Skills C3.1a** or **C3.1b** (see page 6 for details).

Hubris

This means excessive ambition, or arrogance, and it is this flaw which has a bearing on the downfall of the tragic hero. This arrogance may be a refusal to listen to others or to take their advice. Macbeth's pride ensures that he dies defiantly. Hubris can be identified in all of Shakespeare's tragic heroes.

Catastrophe

This is the outcome of hubris and hamartia and is generally the climax, or poignancy, of the drama. Examples of this would be the killings of Hamlet, Coriolanus and Macbeth, or the suffering of King Lear.

Catharsis

This is the cleansing process, or the tidying up of events, which results in a satisfactory resolution on stage. For example, Macduff kills Macbeth and the throne of Scotland is restored to Malcolm, its rightful possessor. In his dying moments, Hamlet states that Fortinbras should take the throne of Denmark. Both instances shown how order replaces catastrophe.

What is comedy?

The word comes from the Greek word 'komos' meaning merry-making, which sums it up rather well.

Comedy is a drama which makes people laugh and it has a happy ending. The laughs are produced largely as a result of human error, such as mistaken identity, or verbal humour. The romantic comedies of Shakespeare involve young love, such as *Twelfth Night* and *The Taming of the Shrew*, and they generally end in marriage. Think about *A Midsummer Night's Dream* where all the lovers are finally united. There are, of course, confusing mix-ups on stage between lovers: Titania falls in love with Bottom, who has been changed into an ass; and Viola, in *Twelfth Night,* is pursued by another woman who believes that Viola is a man! This is typical comedy. Other Shakespearean examples are, *The Comedy of Errors*, *Much Ado About Nothing* and *As You Like It*.

Satire

Satire is a more vitriolic, or vicious, form of comedy and it, too, has its roots in Ancient Greece. It became popular in the eighteenth century and it makes fun of human nature and social position. Satire has an underlying moral stance in that it exposes weaknesses of vice and folly which it contrasts with an ideal.

The Norman Conquests by Alan Ayckbourn can be seen as a modern satire. It exposes flaws within people's relationships and the sterility of marriage. Other twentieth century comic playwrights include Tom Stoppard and Joe Orton.

Comedy in Tragedy

Humour doesn't have to be confined to a comedy. Tragedies often contain humorous intervals. If you think about the play *Hamlet*, a comic interlude is introduced into the play when Hamlet comes upon the Gravedigger. Actually, this is an extremely tense part of the play. Ophelia is about to be buried in the grave which the gravedigger is excavating and Hamlet doesn't know this. The playful conversation between Hamlet and the Gravedigger is a device to build tension (see page 68). The audience is waiting for the Gravedigger to reveal the truth to Hamlet about who's being buried.

GURU TIP
There are few female tragic heroes. This role is left to the men!

Drama

Practice

Task 1

Look at this extract taken from the opening **soliloquy** to Shakespeare's *Richard III* and spoken by Richard himself before he becomes king. It doesn't matter if you know nothing about the play, it's a valuable exercise to work through a speech and piece together the information which is being given.

> **GURU TIP**
> Remember to read the speech thoroughly a couple of times and make sure that you understand the gist of it. You can jot down ideas as you read through.

Now is the winter of our discontent

Made glorious summer by this sun of York;

And all the clouds that lour d upon our house

In the deep bosom of the ocean buried...

...Grim-visag d war hath smooth d his wrinkled front;

And now, instead of mounting barbed steeds

To fright the souls of fearful adversaries,

He capers nimbly in a lady s chamber

To the lascivious pleasing of a lute.

But I, that am not shap d for sportive tricks,

Nor made to court an amorous looking-glass;

I, that am rudely stamp d, and want love s majesty

To strut before a wanton ambling nymph;

I, that am curtail d of this fair proportion,

Cheated of feature by dissembling Nature,

Deform d, unfinish d, sent before my time

Into this breathing world, scarce half made up,

And that so lamely and unfashionable

That dogs bark at me, as I halt by them;

Why, I, in this weak piping time of peace,

Have no delight to pass away the time,

Unless to spy my shadow in the sun,

And descant on mine own deformity:

And therefore, since I cannot prove a lover

To entertain these fair well-spoken days

I am determined to prove a villain

And hate the idle pleasures of these days.

from *Richard III* by William Shakespeare

Questions about characterisation

- Richard say he's 'determined to prove a villain.' How do you think the plot of the play might be decided by this statement?

- What sort of relationship do you think Richard has established with his audience at this point? Remember to support your ideas with evidence from the text.

Questions on Shakespeare's use of dramatic devices

- Look at the language. Think about dark and light images and, conventionally, what these symbolize. What might this tell you about the shaping of the plot of the play?

- Look at the sustained personification of 'Grim-visag'd War.' What is Richard's attitude to war? Look at both the content of the speech and Richard's use of language, which creates a significant tone.

Task 2

The following is an extract from Ibsen's *A Doll's House* and is taken from the beginning of Act Two.

Nora: (drops the coat again). There s someone coming! (Goes to the door and listens.)

No, it s no one. Of course — no one ll come today, it s Christmas Day. Nor tomorrow. But perhaps — ! (Opens the door and looks out.) No.

Nothing in the letter box. Quite empty. (Walks across the room) Silly, silly.

Of course he won t do anything. It shouldn t happen. It isn t possible. Why, I ve three small children.

The nurse carrying a large cardboard box, enters from the room on the left.

Nurse: I found those fancy dress clothes at last, madam.

Nora: Thank you. Put them on the table.

Nurse: (does so) They re all rumpled up.

Nora: Oh, I wish I could tear them into a million pieces!

Nurse: Why, madam! They ll be all right. Just a little patience.

Nora: Yes, of course. I ll go and get Mrs Linde to help me.

Nurse: What, out again? In this dreadful weather? You ll catch a chill, madam.

Nora: Well that wouldn t be the worst. How are the children?

Nurse: Playing with their Christmas presents, poor little dears. But —

Nora: Are they still asking to see me?

Nurse: They re so used to having their mummy with them.

Nora: Yes, but, Anne-Marie, from now on I shan t be able to spend so much time with them.

from *A Doll's House* by Henrik Ibsen

- Gather together information about Nora in the passage. What do the fancy dress clothes tells us about her, for example? She has a maid, what does this tell us of her social status? What sort of woman might she be? Use the stage directions and her speech as pointers.

- There is clearly a problem in Nora's relationship with her children. From this very brief extract, is it possible to anticipate the root of this?

Key points about drama

- Read your play text several times.
- What **genre** is your play?
- Sort out the main characters.
- **Plot** = opening, conflict, climax, resolution.
- How are the setting, lighting, costume and music significant?
- Look at the stage directions.
- Think about audience response.
- Identify the themes running through the play.
- Find relevant quotations to support statements.
- Think about the sub-plot(s).
- Think about dramatic devices.
- Think about recurrent images.
- How do the characters interconnect?
- Be responsive to the language.

Writing

What will you learn in this section?
→ You'll learn how to prepare systematically for your written work.
→ You'll find out how to organise your thinking and discussions about a text into a coherent and reasoned written response.
→ You'll learn some tips on writing under pressure of time.
→ You'll gradually develop the confidence to write answers in a way which is interesting and satisfying for both you and your reader.

Once you have read the sections on reading prose, poetry and drama, you'll know much of the technical language that you need to be able to write effectively. In this section, you'll learn how to make use of all the interesting ideas you've gathered through your own reading and the discussions you have in class. For many students, discussions are fun and stimulating, but they find it difficult to order their thoughts into the form of an essay.

You'll find that the more you practise writing, the easier it becomes. So every time you're asked to do an essay, do actually try to do it well. It makes writing in exams a lot easier if you've done this sort of thing before.

Here are some useful things you could do to improve the quality of your written responses before your exams:

• Ask for plenty of feedback on each essay that you do. Don't just look straight for your mark or grade; the written comments and verbal feedback from your teacher are far more important in helping you improve your work.

• If the teacher has written a comment which you don't quite understand, ask for an explanation.

• Act on the advice your teacher gives you. If your problem is spelling, check your work meticulously. If there's a comment that more analysis is required, make sure you work at this the next time.

• Exchange essays with friends and proofread each other's work in a helpful way. You'd be surprised how much you can learn in this way.

• Prepare well in advance and don't leave your work until the last minute. It helps, for example, to have a timetable for what you are going to do in preparation for an exam. Remember, you will have to fit in revision for all your other subjects, too.

Now look at the systems and methods that have been set out for you over the next few pages. Remember, all of these are suggestions, most of which have been tried and tested by others. Some things are indispensible, such as keeping notes, reading texts several times and planning your essays. However, many are just ideas, and you will need to pick and choose among them to work out what suits your style of learning best.

Before writing

GURU WEBSITE
Look at the 'Original writing' section on the Guru website for more help:
www.bbc.co.uk/ asguru/english

Here are some important points to remember. Some of these have already been mentioned in the section on reading.

- Always keep up-to-date with your class reading. Homework that's set for reading or thinking about is as important as written homework.

- Know your texts. No one else can do this for you. You can't write convincingly about a text you don't know well.

- Before you write anything, make sure you understand what the question is asking of you.

- Always plan. Don't try to avoid it. It's the most important stage in writing an essay and it's <u>not</u> a waste of your time.

- Leave enough time at the end to proofread your work for any spelling and grammar mistakes.

These points apply to any writing you may have to do on a set text, whether it's for course work, class work, or a timed exam.

Learning to write a good essay is no different to any other skill you want to learn. The more you practise, the more skilled you will become.

Preparing to write

You don't have to do an entire essay to practise. Follow the steps below and they will prepare you for writing your essays.

- Look at some essay questions.

- For each question, work out exactly what the question is asking of you.

- Decide what your personal response is to the question. Keep this in mind to act as your conclusion.

- Do a brainstorm of the topic to glean as many ideas as you can which will serve as evidence to support your conclusion.

- Think about how much of this information you can reasonably include in the time allowed.

- Decide which points are the most important to develop and which points can be given less emphasis.

- Decide in what order you will make your points and number them.

- Find the appropriate quotations from the text to support your point of view.

- Think about your introduction in relation to the points you want to make.

Now you are ready to begin writing your essay.

Although this may seem a long process, with practice it will take no longer than five to seven minutes. Once you know what you're going to write, you can concentrate on how you present your material. It makes sense to concentrate on one thing at a time.

Try doing some sample questions following the steps above. This is a good way to plan for possible questions in a timed exam.

GURU TIP
Examiners recommend that you read all exam texts about four times so you know your way around them thoroughly.

GURU TIP
Remember: good planning is the key to a good essay.

How to make notes

You can't study this subject without making notes, but students often find this a particularly difficult task.

Here are some questions about the process, followed by some tips.

How can I make notes effectively?

How can I make sure that I don't write too much or too little?

Should I write everything down that is discussed in class?

- Keep two sets of notes, those you make in your text and those you make in your English folder. If you're not allowed to annotate your text, write page references in your folder notes to help you remember what the notes referred to.

- Keep your notes dated and in order. This is really important if you want to make less work for yourself later.

- You can't write down everything. Record only the main areas of discussion and establish a system that allows you to make notes and join in the discussion. There are some ideas on how to do this below.

Systems

- Don't try to write in whole sentences. Focus on key words and phrases.

- Use capital letters or underlining to highlight major themes and issues. For example, T for themes or C for character, and one word for the theme or character you're referring to.

- Do use abbreviations such as cd (could), shd (should), e.g. (for example), i.e. (that is), cf. (cross reference). Use whatever works for you, but make sure you know what the abbreviations stand for. Use symbols such as &, +.

Order and access

- Write up your notes coherently as soon as possible. If you leave it for too long, you will forget the details.

- Organise them into headings and sub-headings. Use bullet points, colour coding, or underlining to clarify points.

- Add short, relevant quotations with page references. This will increase your familiarity with the text.

- When you've missed a lesson, ask a reliable classmate to let you copy their notes. This is very important in making sure you haven't missed some key discussions.

What to make notes on

- Anything that needs clarification: ideas, words or images.

- Any new or striking ideas which you want to remember.

- References you want to remember about the structure, literary devices, characters, themes and issues in a text.

- Cross references with other pages in the text, which either compare or contrast with what you are currently reading.

Writing

GURU TIP
Keep it brief. Don't cover the text itself with writing. Use abbreviations or symbols to highlight key ideas. When you reread your text, rub out anything that seems unnecessary.

GURU TIP
Notes are not enough on their own. Use them alongside the texts you have studied. Think about what you have written.

Writing a critical essay

Examiners are looking for an informed personal response. This means that they want evidence to show that you've used both your intelligence and your imagination in your reading. They don't have a preconceived idea of what an answer should be; your answer will be judged on how well they think you've responded to the text and the question.

Before you start writing

1. Know your way round your texts.

This point can't be emphasised enough! You'll have notes made in class, and other students and critics may have given you some excellent ideas but, in the end, it's your insights and your ideas that will interest the examiner. Knowing your texts well allows you to respond with confidence. You'll know what you're talking about.

2. Read the text using all your faculties:

- use all five senses

- use your knowledge and experience

- use your imagination, insight and human sympathies

- use your powers of reasoning and analysis.

3. Remember that books are written to interest and entertain. Your personal response is important.

Develop your ideas, perceptions and judgement by asking questions – **how? what? why? when?** This will help to develop your personal response. Have confidence in your ideas and defend your insights and opinions by finding evidence to support your reading of the texts.

Having a system

Approaching your essays in a systematic way, especially when working within a time limit, is really important. By following a method, you can check for yourself that you have covered all the important points you need to make, that you have actually answered the question, and that you have presented your ideas in a coherent and meaningful way. This is the best way to avoid panic.

Here's a strategy to help you organise your essays. The examples used here relate to *Hamlet* by William Shakespeare. If you're not familiar with the play, a summary of it is given on page 82.

1. The title
The title of the essay means the question being asked. Generally, there are two types of question:

a) The direct question:

In your opinion, is Claudius merely, as Hamlet claims, a smiling, damned villain ?

b) The invitation to discuss:

Hamlet says Frailty! thy name is woman . How far do you think this applies to Gertrude and Ophelia?

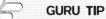

GURU TIP
If you know your text well, you'll find it easier to form opinions about them. Each time you reread a text something new will suggest itself to you.

GURU TIP
Be systematic. Keep your notes up-to-date and in order. It's not enough just to have a system, you've got to use it.

Most essays don't require a definite 'Yes' or 'No' answer, even when the question is direct. It's perfectly acceptable to answer in a way which demonstrates that the answer is more complex than that. Examiners expect you to be aware that texts, characters and events can be read or interpreted in different ways. There is seldom a clear-cut answer to direct questions.

- Begin by underlining the key words in the question and exploring precisely what they mean. This has been done for you, with regard to the first question, in the box below.

> <u>In your opinion</u>, is <u>Claudius merely</u>, as Hamlet claims, a <u>'smiling, damned villain</u>'? Here the key words ask for 'your opinion' on whether 'Claudius' is, as Hamlet claims, a 'villain'.

- Taking the first question again, it seems to require a direct answer, but, in fact, it's inviting you to take into account the evidence presented by events and other characters in the play that may suggest a different picture of Claudius.

- Then, having taken all the evidence into consideration, you are invited to give your judgement on Claudius's character. This may agree with Hamlet's view, or you might conclude that Claudius has some redeeming qualities that make him more than just a villain. Be confident in your reading and demonstrate that you understand the complexity of a character, situation or event.

- Next, put down anything at all that you think is relevant: quotations, events, descriptions. Don't worry about the order. Keep it brief, a word or a phrase to remind you of each idea.

- Reread the question. Look at the words you've underlined. Do your notes add up to an overall answer to the question?

2. Decide on your conclusion

Why should you do this?

- This is the point to which the rest of the essay is leading.

- Knowing your conclusion in advance means you'll be able to structure your evidence systematically towards that conclusion.

- It avoids the panic of wondering how to end the essay and the trap of doing it messily and inconclusively.

> You may decide, for example, that you agree with Hamlet that Claudius is a villain. However, you may wish to argue with the word 'merely'. You may feel that despite his villainy and weaknesses as a private individual, there is plenty of evidence in the play to suggest that he is a good King who is respected by his court, and seeks to bring peace to Denmark through diplomacy rather than war.

Deciding this in advance will help you to shape your evidence accordingly. See more about how to do this on the next page.

KEY SKILLS

Coursework essays give you an ideal opportunity to meet the criteria for **C3.2** 'read and synthesise information from two extended documents about a complex subject' and **C3.3** 'write two different types of documents about complex subjects'. Remember to keep all the notes you make on a subject.

KEY SKILLS

When you're looking for evidence to support your written arguments you might think about using Internet sources. If you do this, you could meet the **Key Skills** criteria for **IT3.1** 'plan and use different sources to search for and select information required for two different purposes'.

79

3. Pick an opening

Make sure that this is relevant and specific. You need to demonstrate two things:

- That you've understood the question.
- That you're able to relate it to the text.

> If the essay title uses a quotation, for example, show how you recognise it in context: here is the opening line of a student essay in response to the same question as before:
>
> *It is not surprising that Hamlet should find Claudius a 'smiling, damned villain'. This is the man who has murdered his father and married his mother. We cannot expect Hamlet to give us an objective, unbiased opinion of his uncle, yet it is possible to read his character as being more than just an 'adulterate beast' and a 'bloat king'.*

> If the question suggests a point of view with which you disagree, (for example, 'Frailty! thy name is woman') try to start by noting the circumstances in which it might be justifiable to hold this opinion (Hamlet's mother has been unfaithful to his father, and Ophelia, having once encouraged him, now seems to be rejecting him). Once you have established a viewpoint from which the judgement makes sense, go on to show how your own opinion is different by presenting alternative evidence.

4. Planning the rest

- Take all the material from stage 1 (page 78).
- Use brackets to group ideas that seem to go together.
- Decide which ideas are important and need to be emphasised.
- Number them in the order in which you think they should be presented. This will make the divisions between paragraphs clearer.
- Think about what quotations to use. This is the evidence to support your reading.

5. Start writing

- Try to stick to your plan.
- Link the paragraphs so that one idea follows another fluently.
- Support your views with evidence and analysis.
- Don't stop until you've finished. Does your conclusion round off your arguments and state your answer to the question clearly?

6. Proofread your answer

Check your work for spelling mistakes, grammar and meaning.

GURU TIP

Remember, the planning stage should take no more than five to seven minutes. If it takes longer, you're writing too much.

GURU TIP

Remember:
1. point of view;
2. evidence and/or a quotation
3. analysis.

Things to remember

You're turning opinions into literary criticism, so you will need to:

- Persuade the reader your views are worth taking seriously.

- Use supporting evidence in the form of short, relevant quotations.

- A quotation by itself is not enough, it should be followed by an analysis. This is not a repetition of the point, but an explanation of how the quotation supports your point of view.

Things to avoid

These are some of the commonest errors in essays.

- **Narrative** response (telling the story). The reader already knows the story and the author will have told it better than you can.

- Using words like 'obviously', as in, 'Hamlet is obviously not mad.' If it was obvious, there would be no need to discuss it.

- Unspecific openings. 'This is a difficult question with many issues involved in it.'

- Following a quotation with a translation. The reader will know the meaning, for example, '"Frailty! thy name is woman" means women are weak creatures.'

- Irrelevance. Try not to pour out all you know about the text without any specific aim. Keep your mind firmly on the question. You should be able to demonstrate that you know what to leave out as well as what to put into your essay.

- Incorrect reference to texts. Don't call a play a book. Plays have audiences and books have readers. With plays, refer to acts and scenes; with novels to chapters; with poems to lines. Don't refer to page numbers as these are often different depending on the edition.

- Don't try to pass off the work of a critic as your own writing. It's good to show you have read widely, and as long as you show where, and from whom, you've borrowed a quote, this is acceptable.

Using quotations

- Quote accurately, keeping quotations short. Try weaving them into a sentence while taking care of the **syntax** (word order), for example:

> Despite his many good qualities as a King, Claudius could best be defined by one particular characteristic – his over-riding self-interest. Although he is racked by guilt, 'How smart a lash that speech doth give my conscience', he will not give up either his ill-gotten crown or his Queen. His love for Gertrude seems to be genuine, 'I could not but by her', but his warning to her in the final scene, 'do not drink', shows that even the possibility of her death cannot displace his self-interest. When she drinks the poison, he says in an aside, 'It is the poison'd cup; it is too late', but rather than draw attention to his guilt, he allows her to drink it, knowing that it will kill her.

- If you are quoting verse at length, quote in lines, as they are in the poem.

- When using a longer quotation, start on a fresh line and indent it.

- As a general guide, any quotation of over four lines is probably too long.

You'll write excellent critical essays if you know the text, plan the answer, trust your judgement, gather the evidence and present the arguments clearly and persuasively.

GURU TIP
There are no 'right answers' in English, although it is possible for answers to be so far off the point of the question or text that they are considered 'wrong'. What examiners are looking for is informed personal response.

Hamlet: a summary

GURU TIP

Remember: a summary is <u>not</u> an acceptable substitute for reading the actual play.

Prince Hamlet has been recalled from his studies to attend the funeral of his father. He is the son of the King of Denmark, who had defeated the King of Norway in battle many years ago. On his return, he finds his mother, Gertrude, has hastily remarried his father s brother, Claudius, who is now installed as the new King of Denmark.

Hamlet is visited by his father s ghost, who reveals to his son that Claudius has murdered him. The Ghost demands that Hamlet should avenge his death, but instructs him to spare his mother.

While Hamlet debates whether or not Claudius is guilty and whether he should kill him, he adopts a disguise by pretending to be mad. However, at times the pressure of what he has to do is such, that the audience is often unclear how far the madness is a disguise or whether it has become a reality. During the course of the play, his behaviour becomes increasingly erratic in his dealings, not only with Claudius, but also with his mother Gertrude, and with Ophelia, a woman he once loved, but who now rejects him on the the instructions of her father. As Hamlet has declared his intention to put an antic disposition on , we are not at first concerned with his sanity. As Polonius, the father of Ophelia and the King s right-hand man, says early in the play, Though this be madness, yet there is method in t , suggesting that Hamlet cannot be entirely mad. However, there are moments in the play when we might doubt this.

Hamlet arranges the performance of a play, which presents as its plot the crimes of his uncle and the adultery of his mother, in order to trap the King into betraying his guilt. Despite the evidence of guilt, Hamlet fails to kill Claudius when he is praying shortly afterwards. He rages against his mother for her unfaithfulness and accidentally kills Polonius who is spying on them, believing it to be Claudius.

Claudius sends Hamlet to England with Rosencrantz and Guildenstern, who carry letters to the English King ordering that Hamlet be put to death. Meanwhile, Ophelia goes mad as a result of her father s death and the loss of her beloved Hamlet, and she drowns herself. Her brother, Laertes, returns from France, swearing vengeance on Hamlet.

Hamlet escapes and returns to Denmark. Claudius encourages Laertes to fight Hamlet in a fencing match. He tries to ensure Hamlet s death by providing Laertes with a poisoned sword and preparing a poisoned drink. Hamlet is wounded but he manages to wound Laertes fatally. Laertes then tells him of the King s treachery. Meanwhile, Gertrude drinks the poison prepared for Hamlet and dies. Hamlet then stabs the King and forces him to drink the poison. Hamlet dies too. His friend, Horatio, is left to observe the entry of Fortinbras of Norway, the son of Denmark s old, defeated enemy, who marches in to take control in the final scene.

Writing for a timed exam

Here are some tips on facing exams and writing essays against the clock. First of all, remember that:

- examiners are just normal people. They have taken exams themselves and know what it feels like.

- they may have students or children of their own who have taken or are about to take exams, so they know how stressful it can be.

- they know that you have to write to a time limit.

- they have an open mind to different viewpoints and readings.

- they want to mark fairly.

They are on your side and will give you the marks if they can find the logic, the arguments and the supporting evidence in your essays.

A ten point plan for timed essays

1. **Revise effectively and know your texts**. Don't just re-read notes and essays, re-read your texts, too.

2. **Target the precise words used in the question** and try not to lose sight of them throughout the answer. It is not enough to refer to it at the beginning and the end, leaving the reader to make the connections.

3. **Plan your essay**. Divide your time carefully between all the questions and keep an eye on the clock as you write. Never answer your question without a plan, however pressed you are for time.

4. **Write legibly**. The examiner has a huge number of essays to mark and won't have time to try and figure out what the squiggles on the page might be saying.

5. **Address the question directly**. Don't waste time with an overlong and rambling introduction.

6. **Support your arguments**. As you write, try to develop your point of view. Whenever you make a point, support it with a quotation and analysis.

7. **Know your subject terminology**. Make sure you have learnt any new terms introduced in class so that you can use a wide vocabulary accurately. Don't be lazy about using a dictionary before the exams.

8. **Be precise**. Don't confuse readers with long, unnecessarily complex sentences. They shouldn't have to guess what you are trying to say, or be allowed to lose the thread of the argument. Don't repeat points and don't use words whose meaning you are not quite sure of. Make your points clearly.

9. **Make each sentence count**. You shouldn't have to start a new sentence because you know the previous one was too vague to make your point.

10. **Be confident** in your own knowledge and judgement.

Key points about writing

Note-taking

- Keep notes brief and in order.

- Use them together with your text.

- Make sure you follow a system for note-taking.

- Rub out any unnecessary notes in your text as your reading makes you more familiar with the text.

- Remember to cross-reference with other pages. This is very useful for sequencing quotations.

Before you start writing

- Know your way round your text.

- Make sure you have developed your ideas.

- Be secure in your perceptions by finding evidence to support your point of view.

- Provided you have found the evidence to support your ideas, be confident about expressing them with conviction. Take your ideas seriously.

Planning

- This is the most crucial stage of the essay. Don't try to save time by avoiding this, it's essential.

- Make sure that your plans add up. They should focus on what is being asked in your title.

- Remember to take particular care in getting your introduction and conclusion right.

Writing

- Try to keep your attention focused while you are writing. Keep your pen moving.

- Remember to keep a link between your ideas. An essay should read fluently, with each paragraph being convincingly connected to the last.

- Keep your quotations short and to the point.

- Always remember to analyse the quotation.

- Try and express yourself clearly and make each sentence count.

- Know your critical terminology and use it.

Avoid

- Irrelevance

- **Narrative** responses

- Incorrect references to texts

- Expressing the view of a critic or teacher that you have not understood and assimilated.

Finally

- Make sure you make the time to proofread your essay at the end for careless mistakes.

Language

What will you learn in this section?
→ You'll learn about systematic language frameworks.
→ You'll learn some grammatical terms and structures.
→ You'll learn about semantics, phonology and spoken language.
→ You'll look at the relationship between language and new technology and between language and advertising.

This section will introduce you to how language is studied. This is very important when you are studying aspects of English Language at AS Level and will provide you with an advanced set of concepts and frameworks that build on the ones you used at GCSE.

Exploring language can be an exciting opportunity to examine a whole range of texts and to gain a greater understanding of the many ways in which language is used.

In your AS English Language and Literature course you will be encouraged to develop your ability to use linguistic concepts and language frameworks to comment on many forms of language, both spoken and written.

You will also look more closely at language in specific contexts – at the language of new technologies and the language of advertising.

At the end of the section there are a number of practice tasks which will give you a chance to try writing for different audiences.

Language frameworks

As AS Level students of English Language and Literature, you need to:

- look at the factors which underpin the structure of language
- understand the main levels on which language operates.

You can think of language as a set of signals by which people communicate. Human language is used to communicate both vocally (speaking) and through written signs (writing). For the purposes of studying language, either a written piece or a spoken piece of language is referred to as a text.

Language and context

TEXT

| Can be spoken or written | Is a vehicle, conveying meaning | Can be literary such as a poem, play or novel | Can be non literary such as a leaflet or ticket |

A text is a vehicle for conveying meaning. Language is used to communicate ideas, thoughts and emotions to an audience. In other words, there is purpose behind every text. When you look at a text you should begin by asking some of the following questions:

- What is the **genre** of the text?
- Who is the audience for the text?
- What is the purpose of the text?

Audience

Look closely at the texts here and on the next page, then try to answer the questions below them.

GURU TIP

A text can be read, it can be heard, and it can consist of:

- sound alone
- written text alone
- a combination of visual images, the written word and audio.

GURU TIP

For more on genre, look at the Prose section on pages 20–25.

Class	Ticket type		Adult	Child	
STD	SAVER RETURN		ONE	NIL	RTN
	Date		Number		
	08 JLY 00		69179	3582e1555M06	
From			Valid		Price
LEICESTER· ✳		SEE RESTRICTIONS			£34·50Q
To			Route		
LONDON TERMINALS					1238

CHOCOLATE AND VANILLA ICE-CREAM CROISSANTS

Enough for 4 as a snack

4 light and flaky croissants
8 small balls of vanilla ice-cream
the Sweet, Shiny Chocolate Sundae Sauce on page 288

Split the croissants in half horizontally and warm them under the grill or in the oven. Place the ice-cream on the bottom halves, then drizzle over the warm chocolate sauce and cover with the remaining halves of the croissantts

when it comes to drugs, the best thing to take is our number.

national drugs helPline 0800 77 66 00

Call us free for advice, help, or just a talk. Calls are confidential.

►►| RADIO 1 INVITE YOU TO

The Nice Girls' RnB Anthems

Sunday 4 April (Doors 7pm)
THE SOUND REPUBLIC
10 Wardour Street - London W1

ADMISSION FREE (NO ENTRANCE WITHOUT TICKET)

BROADCAST LIVE ON RADIO 1
10pm TO MIDNIGHT (MUST BE IN VENUE BEFORE 9:30pm)

DRESS CODE SMART

► **ONE LOVE**

97-99 FM B B C RADIO 1

TERMS & CONDITIONS FOR YOUR
GAS
SUPPLY

British Gas

Spend a few minutes looking at each of the texts above and on the previous page, in turn. When you have done this, begin by asking yourself the following questions about their audience:

- Are there any clues in the language to show what age group is being targeted? For example, reference to specific vocabulary might suggest a target audience of teenagers, or older householders.

- Is the language gender-specific? In other words, is the language aimed at a male or female audience?

- Are there any clues in the language or the layout that would make you think that the text is aimed at a certain social group, such as professional people on a high income, or low-income families?

- Is one person being targeted, or many?

Writers need to know who their writing is for in order to make decisions about the language they will use.

The purpose of a text

When you have decided on the audience of a text, next think about its purpose. In order to identify the purpose in a written or speech-based text, you need to ask yourself which of the following functions the writing performs through the use of language. What does it aim to do?

- argue a point?
- discuss or express an opinion?
- entertain?
- inform?
- instruct?
- persuade?

These are the key elements you need to be aware of when commenting on a text. By asking these questions you can begin to understand how language creates meaning.

What is a language framework?

If you look at these two phrases,

| Late be don't | | Don't be late |

it is obvious to you that **Late be don't** doesn't make much sense, but **Don't be late** gives a clear message. The *order* in which the words are used is very important. People usually take for granted the complex structures which underpin the language they use and allow them naturally to put words in the right order for meaning. You are very familiar with the spoken and written language that you use in everyday life without really being aware of it.

Young children instinctively learn the rules of language as they grow. However, in order to be able to discuss and analyse these aspects of language, you need 'tools' to help you label and define each detail within a text, and for this you use a language framework. A language framework provides you with ways to look at a language's rules, origins, complexities and functions.

There are examples throughout this section of the book to show you how you might apply the frameworks in the English exam.

Linguistics

You may have come across the term Linguistics before. The most common definition of Linguistics is 'the scientific study of language', and what Linguists aim to do is to study language systematically.

They observe how people use language by creating models and frameworks to analyse the different ways people speak and write, and the way both of these 'modes', as they are called, are used to communicate and create meaning.

Grammar

Grammar is the study of the component parts of language and how they fit together. David Crystal, a professor of linguistics, says grammar is the way in which you can begin to understand language and the meanings that are created:

> Grammar is what gives sense to language.... Sentences make words yield up their meaning. Sentences actively create sense in language. And the business of the study of sentences is grammar.

You could say that grammar is like a corset under a dress – it holds up the language even though you cannot see it. If the 'grammar' was removed, the text would be hard to follow. The next section of the book explains a number of grammatical terms and shows you why grammatical structures are so important in the communication of English.

Language framework diagram

The diagram below outlines the ways in which you can define language.

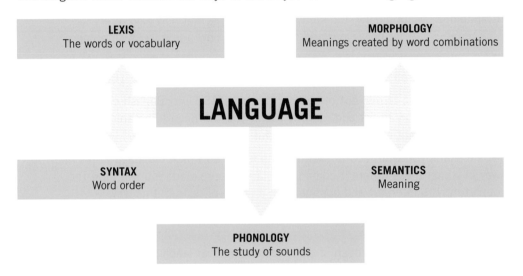

GURU WEBSITE
Check out the definitions on this language framework diagram on the AS Guru website:
www.bbc.co.uk/asguru/english

The purpose of language

Through studying the use of language, and its interpretation, you can see how people communicate with each other. Written language offers the opportunity to communicate with others you might not know:

- they might live in different places,
- be from other cultures,
- or even from a different time.

Writing is more permanent than speech and, therefore, must follow certain sets of rules.

By understanding the main grammatical terms and structures within which language operates, you can obtain a framework which can be used to analyse the language around you.

Rules, such as those for spelling and grammar, help authors to communicate their intentions. They can transmit their opinions or knowledge to others in a clear and consistent way, knowing that the reader will understand the specific message that they want to convey.

GURU TIP
Don't expect to discuss *every* feature in the list opposite for *every* text.

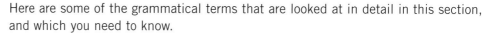

GURU TV
David Crystal, Professor of Linguistics, takes you on a guided tour of phonology in the TV programmes.

GURU WEBSITE
The language section of the AS Guru™ website has more information on lexis: www.bbc.co.uk/asguru/english

Here are some of the grammatical terms that are looked at in detail in this section, and which you need to know.

Lexis	the study of words and vocabulary. (See below.)
Morphology	the study of the structure of words. (See page 92.)
Syntax	is the study of the structure of sentences. (See page 93.)
Semantics	is the study of the meanings of words. (See page 98.)
Phonetics	is the study of the sound systems of languages. (See page 100.)

It is also interesting to think about:

Orthography	the study of how words are spelt.
Graphology	originally, the study of handwriting, but now also refers to design, layout and typeface – or how a text looks on a page.
Pragmatics	the meanings which are dependent, not on the language alone, but on the setting in which it takes place. (See page 100.)

Try to learn these terms, but remember that your AS Level English course will not require you simply to list and identify them; you will need to be able to use the terms to comment on texts in a meaningful way.

In the exam, you will need to examine the levels on which language works and the way in which these different components are inter-related. You will have the opportunity to interpret and comment on a range of texts in this way.

Lexis

The **lexis** of English has been steadily increasing ever since people began speaking to each other. An Anglo-Saxon would have used words which relate to everyday life – house, man, beer – and other words were added as human knowledge grew.

The words 'dictionary' and 'printing press' developed in the fifteenth century, for example, when these items were invented.

Shakespeare had a vocabulary of about 30,000 words when he wrote his plays. Four hundred years later, there are over 300,000 words in the English language and more are being added all the time.

Word formation
Words enter the language from a number of sources. They can be:

1. Created from bits of other words, in the different ways shown below.

- **Compounds** are created by joining two existing words together: key+board (keyboard); web+site (website); lap+top (laptop).

  Compounds can be:

  – solid (soundbite),

  – hyphenated (match-winner),

  – or open (ice cream).

- **Acronyms** are new words created from the initial letters of a phrase. For example:
  - AIDS, Acquired Immune Deficiency Syndrome
  - NATO, North Atlantic Treaty Organisation
  - ISA, Individual Savings Account.
- **Conversions** are when a word jumps a class, usually noun to verb, as in telephone. This was originally the name of the machine (a telephone = noun) but came to mean the act of using the telephone (to telephone = verb).
- **Derivations** are words created by adding a bit on the beginning (prefix), middle (infix) or end suffix).

  Inter+net is 'net' plus the prefix 'inter'.

  Two suffix-based derivations are Govern+ment and Blair+ite.

2. **'Borrowed' from other languages**, for example:

restaurant – French

tea – Chinese

coffee – Turkish (from the Arabic word kahwa)

potato – Spanish

3. **Old words recycled with a new meaning**

For example, **mouse**, which now means a computer device as well as a small animal.

4. **Completely original (called coinages)**

These are often dreamed up by advertising executives. Recent coinages include **Hobnobs** and **Ikea**. You'll find hundreds more in any supermarket.

Meanings do change over time. Your study of Shakespeare will have shown you that words aren't used in the same way today as four hundred years ago. This process is called semantic change. It occurs because:

- words die out of use because they are not needed any more (*porringer, pottage*); or are replaced because of fashion (*trainers* has replaced *pumps*).
- New words enter the language, either from various other languages (*pizza, donut, cocoa*), or through invention.
- Words alter to fulfil a new function or gain a new meaning. *Awesome* originally meant something that inspired awe in a person (great fear or wonder, often with religious overtones). Now the word is often used to suggest something was impressive or enjoyable, as in *Awesome party last night!*

Choice of lexis

The most important factor in choosing lexis is audience. The audience also determines how formal the text will be.

In a medical journal, for example, the author would outline the area of study for other scientists to understand. The lexis may well include scientific words and procedures, which may be incomprehensible to readers who do not know the subject.

Similarly, when reading a book which has been written for children, the lexis will be selected for its simplicity. In each case, the audience will affect the choice of lexis. Even when a children's book is aimed at a wider teenage audience, such as J.K. Rowling's series of *Harry Potter* books, the language has been structured so that the audience will recognise the genre as being aimed at a specific age group.

> **GURU TIP**
> See the section on spoken language on page 102 for a diagram of words which have entered the English Language as a result of immigration into Britain over the last fifty years.

Language

> **GURU TIP**
> Look at the Language and new technologies section on page 106 for more on the impact of electronic communication and the development of digital technologies.

> **GURU TIP**
> Etymology is the study of the historical meaning of a word. You could use an etymological dictionary to add to examples of word formation given here.

> **GURU TIP**
> Look at the section on **Semantics** (page 98) for more on audience.

Morphology and syntax

Morphology is the study of the structure of words. A **morpheme** is the smallest unit of language which can convey meaning. The words morphology and morpheme have their origins in the Greek word meaning 'shape' or 'form'. Let's look at some examples. Here are some everyday names of things – <u>nouns</u>.

cat	dog	hat

If we add an 's' to these words the structure will change. The word becomes plural, which indicates that there is more than one. For example,

cats	dogs	hats
Singular	Plural	
cat	cat +s	
dog	dog +s	
hat	hat +s	

These words are made up of two morphemes, the morpheme **cat**, **dog** or **hat** and the morpheme **s**.

Now let's look at some words showing action – **verbs**. What is the function of the morpheme **ed** when added to the morphemes **look** and **walk**?

look	looked
walk	walked

By adding 'ed' it shows that the action is now complete and the verb is in the past tense. You already know that 'ed' is used to indicate the past tense for many verbs in the English language.

Free and bound morphemes

Morphemes which can appear independently are called free morphemes. For example:

> cat, dog, hamster, hat, look, walk, travel...

Morphemes which cannot usually make sense on their own are known as bound morphemes.

Bound morphemes can be divided into two types:

- **prefixes** such as 'un' or 'dis' that precede free morphemes (**un**happy, **dis**trust)
- **suffixes** such as 'ness', 'ly', 'ed' and 's' that come after free morphemes (sad**ness**, love**ly**).

Some words are made up of a number of morphemes:

> **deconstruction** = de + construct + ion
> **reconsidered** = re + consider + ed

The morphemes each do a different job within the final word. Free and bound morphemes are dependent on each other to make sense, even though the free morphemes *seem* to carry the meaning more.

Allomorphs

Allomorph is the term used to describe a group of morphemes which do the same job. For example, if you want to make something negative, you can use:

> **in-** (**in**sensitive), **im-** (**im**proper) or **il-** (**il**legal)
>
> **in-**, **im-** and **il-** are allomorphs.

GURU TIP
Look at page 94 for more on nouns and verbs.

GURU TIP
See the section on **Semantics** (page 98) which will tell you how the meaning of words is created.

GURU WEBSITE/TV
Check out the language section on the AS GuruTM website and TV programmes for more information on morphology and syntax:
www.bbc.co.uk/asguru/english

What is syntax?

Syntax is the study of the way sentences are structured. When you produce a sentence, all the different elements in it must appear in a certain order for the language to make sense.

It would be very confusing if any combination of all the available words were just thrown together in an attempt to make meaning. To help organise meaning, you can classify the words that make up clauses, phrases and sentences into word classes, or types. Each word class has a different function, as shown below.

Word classes	Functions
Nouns	naming words, words which label, such as table, tree
Adjectives	words which describe nouns, for example big, white, important
Pronouns	words that replace nouns, such as he, she, it
Verbs	words which describe actions, such as run, walk, be
Adverbs	add information about verbs, for example quickly, excitedly
Prepositions	words which indicate relationships, such as above, out, down
Conjunctions	words which connect parts of speech, such as and, but, because
Articles	can be used before all common nouns, such as the, a, an

The position that a word occupies in a sentence to contribute to the sentence's meaning depends on its class. If you were given a list of words such as:

the went hill I steep up,

you might <u>guess</u> the intended message from the meanings of the individual words, but your innate knowledge of word classes would tell you that they <u>should</u> be arranged:

I	went	up	the	steep	hill
pronoun + verb + preposition + article + adjective + noun					

Clauses and phrases

The words in a sentence are often grouped together into **clauses** and **phrases**.

- A clause is a distinct part of a sentence that includes a subject and a predicate.
- The **predicate** is what is said about the subject (Trees **are green**, All men **are mortal**).
- A co-ordinate **clause** joins two parts of a sentence together. (Apples taste nice **although I really feel that** I prefer oranges.)
- A **phrase** is a short group of words, usually without a predicate, that does the job of an adverb, adjective or noun. (**The castle by the river; I agree to do it**).

Using what you've learnt

> Giving and receiving presents is wonderful. There's nothing like opening a carefully-wrapped package on a birthday or at Christmas to remind you how much your nearest and dearest mean to you. You're grateful for the time that has gone into choosing the gift, purchasing it, tying all those pretty bows on top – but there's a little part of you that is busy calculating the cost of it, wondering whether your true worth has been appreciated.

You would be well rewarded if you wrote:

'The writer uses the subordinate clause, "but there's a little part of you" to demonstrate how mercenary thoughts lie just below the surface.'

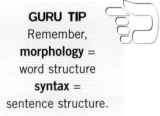

Nouns, adjectives and verbs

Nouns are naming words, which label things. They are the first words that babies learn, to make sense of their surroundings. They form the largest word class.

Nouns can be:

common	city, girl, drink
or **proper**	Manchester, Helen, Pepsi
count	which can be singular or plural, whether in a regular form or not. Book(s) is regular and child(ren) is irregular, but they are both plurals.
or **non-count**	which have no plural forms and take a singular verb (Furniture is in every room).
concrete	which describe things you can see and touch (phone, table, tree)
or **abstract**	which describe feelings (love); ideas (realism); qualities (beauty) and things you cannot touch.

GURU TIP
Proper nouns are those with capital letters.

In this example, the concrete nouns are in bold and the abstract nouns are underlined.

> Having such a great **space** in front of the **house** gave the **children** a <u>feeling</u> of <u>night</u>, of <u>vastness</u>, and of <u>terror</u>. This terror came in from the shrieking of the **tree** and the <u>anguish</u> of the home <u>discord</u>.
>
> from *Sons and Lovers* by D H Lawrence

Adjectives

Adjectives are words which describe nouns.

They can:

- **modify**   add information about nouns

> Coming towards us there s a **small** procession, a funeral: **three** women, each with a **black transparent** veil thrown over her headdress. ...Their **striped** dresses are **worn-looking**.
>
> from *The Handmaid's Tale* by Margaret Atwood

- be **concrete**   give clear, objective information
- or **abstract**   are a matter of subjective opinion

Using the example above, the concrete adjectives are: *three, black, transparent, striped*; the abstract adjectives are *small* and *worn-looking*.

- **be used as many as you like before a noun**

  The *ugly, old, decrepit, dilapidated, frightening* house was haunted.

- **carry bias**   This means they show the prejudices of the user, for example, a politician might say,

  'our *ailing* Health Service' or 'our *admirable* Health Service'

  depending on his or her attitude.

- **be graded**   They can vary in degree of intensity (comparative and superlative).

GURU WEBSITE
There's more on the AS Guru™ website about types of nouns, adjectives and verbs:
www.bbc.co.uk/asguru/english

Comparative and superlative

The adjective *tall* can be interpreted in different ways – it depends who you are standing next to.

Adjectives can take on a **comparative** form (*taller*) and a **superlative** form (*tallest*). Here are some more examples:

sweet, sweeter, sweetest;   *happy, happier, happiest*

The other way to make these forms is to use *more* to form the comparative and *most* to form the superlative, for example:

famous, more famous, most famous;   *expensive, more expensive, most expensive.*

There are also some irregular forms, for example:

good, better, best;   *bad, worse, worst;*   *far, farther, farthest*

Verbs

Verbs are words which describe actions. Sentences don't make sense without one. Verbs can be:

- **in the infinitive form**, which is the base form:

    to write, to run, to work

- **finite**   the verb is broken into usable parts, like this:

    I write, you write, he/she/it writes...

it shows us the **person**, (*I* is different to *he*, for instance),
the **tense (past, present, future** and so on), (*write, wrote, written...*),
and the **number (singular or plural)**, (*he* or *they*, for example).

- or **non-finite** the infinitive is non-finite, because it does not change form.

- **regular**   like the example using *write*, above

- or **irregular**   where the pattern is not followed, for example <u>to be</u>:
    I am, you are, he/she/it is

- **stative**   referring to <u>states</u>, such as *to be, to have, to belong, to know*

- or **dynamic**   referring to <u>actions</u>

In this extract from *The Handmaid's Tale* by Margaret Atwood, the stative verbs are in **bold** and the dynamic verbs are <u>underlined</u>:

*And the Commander, for a change, **is waiting;** I can **hear** him pacing in the main room. Now he <u>pauses</u> outside the bathroom door, <u>clears</u> his throat, a stagy 'ahem'. I <u>turn</u> on the hot water tap... I **should** get this over with. I <u>wash</u> my hands.*

The dynamic verbs make the text much more exciting. Stative and dynamic verbs usually complement each other.

- **divided into main verbs**   which convey significant meaning

- and **auxiliary verbs**   which do a support job and usually go before the main verb.

The student is writing an essay   (*is* = aux, *writing* = main)

The student has written the essay   (*has* = aux, *written* = main)

His friend did not write the essay   (*did* = aux, *write* = main)

The three auxiliary verbs are *to be, to have* and *to do*. They are all irregular.

You will also come across modal auxiliary verbs. They suggest possibility or probability. They are *will/would, can/could, may/might, shall/should,* and *must*.

> **GURU TIP**
> Think about the different nuances in meaning that would be suggested without the auxiliary verbs.

    95

More grammatical terms

Adverbs give extra information, usually about a **verb**.

There are three types of adverb:

GURU TIP

Adverbs are words which specify a kind of action expressed by a verb. They say how, when or where the verb was done.

- **Adverbs of manner** which are easy to spot because they are usually formed from an adjective + **ly**, e.g. quick**ly**, happi**ly**, polite**ly**. (Sometimes you have to take care with the spelling, for example: lazy - laz**ily**, artistic - artistic**ally**)

- **Adverbs of time** which are irregular and tell you about the time an action will take place, for instance *today, tomorrow, next week,* and so on

- **Adverbs of place** which are also irregular and tell you where the action takes place, for example *in the café, on the beach, there,* and so on.

Adverbs can be **comparative**:

> Helen ran _fast_ in her race, but Eva ran _faster_.

And **superlative**:

> Rhiannon was _fastest_ and won in a new record time.

Using what you've learnt

> You must have been studying hard in order to write so nicely. I have been studying too. But I often go out and walk in Luxembourg Gardens, which is a sort of park like the Boston Public Gardens, or the park down the hill from your home in Brookline, where I used to go.
>
> extracts pages 96—97 from a letter by T S Eliot to his six year-old niece, Theodora, from *The Letters of T S Eliot*, edited by Valerie Eliot

You would be well rewarded if you wrote:

> 'Eliot uses the adverb of frequence "often" and the present tense verb "go out and walk" to convey to Theodora that he has time for fun and give her a sense of his typical routines.'

Conjunctions

Conjunctions are words which connect parts of speech. They can connect words or clauses.

Word level: Her new jeans were sleek **and** elegant **and** classy.

Clause level: She called her boyfriend **but** he wasn't in.

Pronouns and deictics

Pronouns stand in for nouns.

The commonest kind are **personal pronouns**:

I, you, he, she, it, we, they, me, us, them, him, her.

They help writers to avoid unnecessary repetition in texts, and create links within the texts.

You can see how important they are if you look at this passage, which uses no personal pronouns at all:

Alec gave Dawn a big bunch of flowers because Alec wanted to say to Dawn that Alec was sorry and Alec wouldn't embarrass Dawn again like Alec had last week.

You will also come across pronoun references, such as **it**, **this** and **that,** which ensure that the listener knows what, where and to whom the language is referring. These words are called **deictics**.

*I bought a jumper last week, but I didn't like **it** so I took **it** back to the shop.*

Using what you've learnt

> Just about now you are having supper in America, and here, it is my bed time. Isn t that funny?

You would be well rewarded if you wrote:

'At the end Eliot uses the adverbs "here" and "now", which are deictic and reflect the nature of letter-writing as a kind of simulated conversation.'

Articles

Articles can be used before all common nouns. They are:

the, a, an.

Using *the* in front of a word identifies it as specific. Think about the difference between these two sentences:

Give me a rose   which implies that there are many roses.

Give me the rose   which implies that there is only one rose.

You can define an article as a word that specifies whether a noun is definite or indefinite.

> **GURU TIP**
> Articles are part of a larger group called determiners. They may be referred to as determiners in your syllabus.

Semantics

GURU WEBSITE
There's a whole section on semantics on the AS Guru™ website:
www.bbc.co.uk/asguru/english

Semantics is concerned with the way in which meaning is created. It is key to the study of language because the whole point of language is to convey meaning, but it's not as easy as that! Who decides what a word means? It depends on the audience. Let's look at some examples:

- If you tell your friends that you went to a *wicked* party last night, would you be implying that it was actually a gathering of evil witches and warlocks – or that you had a great time?

- If an eighteenth century writer described a man as *nice* in his habits, would it be implying that he admired him – or that he was very fastidious and picky?

Of course, the second meaning is what is really meant in each case, but it's easy to see how the meaning could be mistaken if the receiver of the language has a different definition of the word to the one intended.

Connotation and denotation

The dictionary definition of a word is known as its **denotation**. This is the clear, objective, unbiased meaning.

For example, the word 'sea' is defined in the *Concise Oxford English Dictionary* as *'expanse of salt water that covers most of Earth's surface'*. However, if you were a fisherman and earned your living form the sea, the connotational meaning would for you be associated with life on a boat, long days hauling in nets, and danger. If, on the other hand, you were a child about to go on a seaside holiday, the connotational meaning would be associated with paddling and splashing and having fun.

Here's another example:

The colour red carries various **connotations**:
- Danger - red alert
- Anger - seeing red
- Passion - red hot

Think about the connotations that other colours carry.

Semantic fields

When you read a text, you may notice that some words tend to cluster together. Look at these lists:

- hot, fire, flame, burn, scald, scorch, heat
- green, fresh, young, lively, vigour

Although they don't necessarily mean the same thing, (that is, they are not **synonyms** – see below), their individual meanings can all be linked together to form a semantic field.

Use of a semantic field can help reinforce the meaning in both spoken and written texts. Gerard Manley Hopkins, in his poem 'Pied Beauty', uses a semantic field of changing colours to express his wonder in God:

GURU TIP
A semantic field is the deliberate grouping of words with related meaning in a text.

> Glory be to God for dappled things -
> For skies of couple-colour as a brinded cow;
> For rose-moles all in stipple upon trout that swim;
>
> from 'Pied Beauty' by Gerard Manley Hopkins

Synonyms

A **synonym** is a word that means the same as another. However, due to the very nature of language, it could be argued that no one word ever has *exactly* the same meaning as another. A thesaurus is a good place to find possible synonyms.

Writers often use words which could be synonyms to influence meaning. Think about the different effect of this passage if the second of the two synonyms was used in each case:

> *He made his way slowly back to his <u>house/home</u> through the <u>wood/forest</u>. The sun was setting and a vivid <u>amber/orange</u> filled the sky.*

- Is a house the same as a home?
  home generally suggests somewhere warmer and more welcoming than house

- Is amber the same colour as orange?
  amber is precious and glows, while orange might suggest something brighter

- Is a wood the same as a forest?
  a wood is often thought to be less threatening than a forest.

Antonyms

An **antonym** is an opposite.

hot — cold
rich — poor

That's all there is to it! Think how a writer might use antonyms for effect. You might find pairs of antonyms in political speeches, for example, to emphasise a claim that while one party has made the country rich, the policies of another might make it poor (or vice versa).

Hyponomy

The Greek prefix *hypo* means 'under', which is a clue to how it operates. If the meaning of one word is used in the broader meaning of another, it is said to be its **hyponym**.

- a **lily** is a hyponym of flower
- a **4WD** is a hyponym of car

These can be taken to several layers:
building – accommodation – flat – penthouse

The word which has the broadest meaning (flower, car, building) is called the superordinate.

Collocation

This comes from Latin: *collocatio* means putting two or more things together. Here, it refers to the in-built associations native speakers of a language apply to particular pairs of words. The native speakers use them instinctively, but they can be very difficult for non-native speakers to master. Some examples are:

- Salt and pepper
- Bucket and spade
- Sky blue

GURU TIP
Look at the poetry section for information on figurative language and imagery.

GURU TIP
Look at the section on lexis (page 90) to give you more information about words changing.

Language

Phonetics and pragmatics

The study of sounds made by the human voice is known as phonetics. Phonetics is concerned with both articulated sounds (the sounds which are spoken) and auditory sounds (those which are heard).

All languages make use of vowels and consonants, but no two languages are made up of the same set of distinct sounds. Although there are 26 letters in the English alphabet, there are 44 sounds – **phonemes** – in the British English phonology system. For example, **t** and **h** are distinct sounds, but **th** is a different sound altogether. **t**, **h** and **th** are therefore all phonemes as each phoneme represents a different sound.

The International Phonetic Alphabet (IPA)

When phoneticians discuss phonetics, they use the IPA (rather than just ordinary spelling), as it enables them to represent phonemes precisely.

Study the chart on the opposite page which shows the IPA. You don't need to memorise this chart, but it is interesting to take a closer look and see how it is used. You will find examples of each of the sounds in the English Language.

- The IPA is seen as a regular and consistent way of describing the sounds that appear in speech.

- Twenty of the phonemes in the IPA are vowel sounds.

- The alphabet is based on the Roman alphabet, but has been supplemented with additional symbols so that all of the sounds can be represented accurately.

- Transcripts often use sets of sound symbols taken from the IPA. If you look in a dictionary, you will see that the IPA is used as a guide to pronunciation.

Pragmatics

Pragmatics is a difficult term to define because it is so closely linked to the other linguistic frameworks. David Crystal (*Cambridge Encyclopaedia of Language*) quotes, 'How's tricks, your Majesty?' as an example. Technically, it's not wrong, but its language breaks many social conventions. This involves the study of Pragmatics.

Another way of looking at it is to say, it's about decoding meaning. Pragmatics is the study of the difference between what you mean to say and the words you chose to say it in. Let's look at some examples:

- You might say to a friend, 'You've got a new outfit,' which sounds neutral, but you might mean, 'You look terrible in it.'

- Your teacher might write in your report, 'You have trouble meeting deadlines,' but you know she actually means, 'You haven't handed in a single homework on time all year.'

- Mrs Thatcher said in a speech when she was elected Prime Minister, 'The way will be hard.' Some commentators might say that she actually meant, 'Everyone is going to suffer increased taxation.'

Comedy often relies on pragmatics. A favourite playground joke is, 'Why is a chef a vicious person?' The answer is, 'Because he beats eggs and whips cream!' The answer relies on a literal interpretation of the words beats and whips, but a different literal interpretation from the one suggested by the question.

GURU TIP
Look at the phonetic spelling of an entry in a dictionary and see if you can work out which word it represents.

GURU TIP
The next section tells you more about the study of spoken language.

GURU TV
There's a section in the TV programmes about Pragmatics.

GURU TIP
Check the poetry section for details on alliteration, assonance, consonance, rhythm and rhyme, which are all to do with sounds.

In Literature, writers use pragmatics to give their characters 'voices'. Edmund Blunden, a war poet, in his poem 'Premature Rejoicing', presents us with an army officer who says,

'That's where the difficulty is, over there',

when he actually means,

'That's where the enemy is and it's a very dangerous situation.'

The choice of language you use in a particular context is an example of pragmatics. For example, when speaking to the Head Teacher of your school you might not say,

'How's it going, mate'?

but you might say

'Good afternoon, Sir'.

As context and the process of social interaction affect the language you use to communicate ideas, thoughts and feelings, you can see how the study of pragmatics is useful in the study of language.

GURU WEBSITE
Find out more about phonology and pragmatics by looking at the AS Guru™ website: www.bbc.co.uk/ asguru/english

Language

List of the International Phonetic Alphabet

The consonant sounds of English are:					
/p/	as in **p**art	/f/	as in **f**ood	/h/	as in **h**as
/b/	as in **b**ut	/v/	as in **v**oice	/m/	as in **m**at
/t/	as in **t**oo	/θ/	as in **th**ing	/n/	as in **n**ot
/d/	as in **d**id	/ð/	as in **th**is	/ŋ/	as in lo**ng**
/k/	as in **k**iss	/s/	as in **s**ee	/l/	as in **l**et
/g/	as in **g**et	/z/	as in **z**oo	/r/	as in **r**ed
/tʃ/	as in **ch**in	/ʃ/	as in **sh**e	/j/	as in **y**es
/dʒ/	as in **j**oke	/ʒ/	as in mea**s**ure	/w/	as in **w**ill

The vowel sounds of English are:					
(long vowels)		(short vowels)		(diphthongs)	
/ɪː/	as in **ea**ch	(ɪ)	as in **i**t	/eɪ/	as in d**ay**
/ɑː⁽ʳ⁾/	as in c**ar**	/e/	as in th**e**n	/aɪ/	as in b**y**
/ɔː⁽ʳ⁾/	as in m**ore**	/æ/	as in b**a**ck	/ɔɪ/	as in b**oy**
/uː/	as in t**oo**	/ʌ/	as in m**u**ch	/əʊ/	as in n**o**
/ɜː⁽ʳ⁾/	as in w**ord**	/ɒ/	as in n**o**t	/aʊ/	as in n**ow**
		/ʊ/	as in p**u**t	/ɪə⁽ʳ⁾/	as in n**ear**
		/ə/	as in ag**ai**n	/eə⁽ʳ⁾/	as in th**ere**
				/ʊə⁽ʳ⁾/	as in tr**uer**

The small ' r' indicates what is known as r-controlled vowels (that is, they blend with an 'r' sound). The slanting lines represent a phoneme.

Spoken language

For English Language and English Language and Literature at AS Level you need to show an understanding of spoken language texts.

Differences between spoken and written texts

- Spoken language depends on there being a listener to receive the message. The pattern of thought is constructed by the speaker and interpreted by the listener.

- Spoken language isn't always as planned and ordered as a written text. If you listen to someone talking you might hear hesitation, repetition and casual and colloquial words thrown in. Written texts, on the other hand, are often drafted, re-written and edited, and are altogether more polished.

- In spoken communication, the speaker's gestures, facial expressions, accent and pronunciation, pace and volume may also be very important.

To illustrate this point, read the following extracts; one of them is written and the other is a transcript of spoken language. They both deal with the same topic of a school environmental project.

Cool School

Guardian Education Tuesday July 11 2000

The fruit trees in a London orchard are getting some TLC from an unlikely source

Where school is a bowl of cherries

... La Sainte Union is an 11-18 state convent school in Camden fortunate enough to have an orchard within the school grounds, belonging to the neighbouring convent. Britain's orchards are in a state of rapid decline, with 150,000 acres lost over the past 40 years. The school's orchard was dangerously close to being lost, too, but thanks to the initial impetus of the National Orchards Campaign and with the help of the charity Common Ground, the girls at the school began the hard work of restoring it in January 1999.

Nancy O'Brien, the teacher in charge, remembers that of the 68 trees in the orchard, some planted 150 years ago, only three were producing fruit when the project began...

Presenter Lucy Alexander is talking to Dan Keech from Common Ground about the need to preserve Britain's orchards.

Presenter: Dan, why is it so important that we save our orchards?

Dan: Well, orchards I think contribute, er, to a great deal, to many elements of our, er, countryside and towns as well. Er, when old orchards are lost, em, standard trees are very, er, widely spaced...

A good starting point would be to examine the following areas, which distinguish spoken language from the written form:

- mode of address
- register
- intonation
- tone
- accent and **dialect**.

These are discussed in more detail on the next three pages.

Mode of address

When you look at spoken language, you will come across the term 'mode of address'. This refers to the level of informality or formality in a spoken text. When people speak, issues such as status, gender, cultural diversity and age may affect the way in which they talk to, or address, each other.

Consider spoken language in two genres of television programme.

Chat shows aimed at young people will be 'fronted' by a particular kind of speaker:
- the presenters may speak very quickly
- they may speak with a regional accent
- they may move around the set while speaking.

News broadcasts use a different style:
- the presenters will speak slowly and clearly
- they will often speak with Received Pronunciation (RP)
- the shot will always be 'head and shoulders' and the speaker will speak directly to the camera, which implies authority.

These features are intentional and this mode of verbal and non-verbal address is used in order to appeal to the different audiences. Imagine the response if the person reading the evening news spoke in a dialect, using colloquial language and slang, and if the presenter of a youth programme spoke in a formal tone.

To put it another way, would you use the same mode of address when chatting to a friend as you would during the interview for a job or a place at your first-choice university?

Register

Register is the term that linguists use to describe the way in which language is affected by context and situation.

Contexts which affect register include:

- The purpose of the language. For example, it may be:
  - to express an opinion
  - to convey information
  - to persuade or entice.
- The social relationships of the participants – is the tone formal or informal?
- Where the language is taking place.

Different language contexts have developed their own characteristic registers and specific vocabulary. For example;
- religious ceremonies
- the legal profession
- sporting commentaries
- on-line entertainment.

All use specialist vocabulary to describe terms which are specific to them. You could add lots more categories to that list.

To give an example, two people eating in a restaurant may be familiar and speak on a personal and familiar level. However, an exchange between one of the guests and a waiter may be more impersonal as the two people will be strangers. The context will affect the tone of the exchange. The relationships between the people who are communicating in a given context will affect the register.

GURU TIP
Received Pronunciation (RP) is the name for the accent derived from the educated English spoken in the South East of England.

Language

GURU TIP
Modes of address in spoken language are chosen to ensure that the intended audience is targeted.

GURU TIP
Differences in register involve differences in grammar and vocabulary.

Intonation and accents

Intonation is the rhythm and the 'tune', or the rise and the fall, of a person's voice. The individual sounds of the human range are rather like music. Intonation is a feature often recognised and used by users of language, from poets to politicians, who use rhythm and variation in intonation to produce an effect.

Think back to the example on page 103 and imagine the differences in intonation between the host of a chat show and a newsreader.

Tone

You have already looked at the importance of tone in literature as a device for creating character, mood and atmosphere and the way in which the reader interprets the writer's intent. (See page 28)

The tone of the text can help you to understand the position of the speaker and the relationship between the listener and the speaker.

• If you were to make a telephone call to book a ticket for the cinema, the exchange would be formal and the telephone booking agent might say, 'Good afternoon, Sir, how can I help you?' The tagging of 'Sir' on the end of a question is a marker of social distance.

• If you were to phone a friend, he might greet you by saying, 'Hi mate, how you doing?' There is clearly a more familiar and informal relationship between the speaker and the person being addressed here.

In other words, the tone used is appropriate to the situation.

Look at the script below, which is taken from a news broadcast. What do you notice about the tone of the language in the text?

> Reports from Latvia say there s been an explosion in a big department store in the capital, Riga. Initial reports say at least twelve people were hurt at the centre s store, and that there were two blasts, one coming shortly after the other. It s not known if there was a bomb. Details are still coming in.
>
> *BBC World Service news script*

The use of specific vocabulary and phrases (*Reports from..., Initial reports say...*) and the inclusion of precise details imply that the text should be read in a formal tone, which would suggest authority.

Accent and dialect

Another important area of spoken language is accent and dialect. When you listen to the language around you, have you noticed that many of the people who live in your area pronounce words in a similar way.

bath = **bath** (with a short a) or **barth**?

There are many words which are pronounced differently depending on which part of the country you live in. So, how do you define accent and what is the difference between accent and dialect? It's easy to confuse the two terms, so try to remember these basic definitions:

GURU WEBSITE
There's more information on accents and dialogue on the AS Guru™ website:
www.bbc.co.uk/asguru/english

AS Guru™ English

- Accent: sound variations according to place. Neighbours is set in Australia and its characters speak English with an Australian accent.
- **Dialect**: regional variations of sound, grammar and vocabulary. Different words and grammatical structures may be heard in a dialect, which are not used by other speakers of the language – it's more than just pronunciation.

Languages, dialects and accents are in a continual state of flux. This is caused by the influences upon people such as migration, mobility, lifestyle, and technological factors, such as television. Migration is the key factor in the development of the Liverpudlian, or Scouse, accent. As a port, Liverpool has seen many people come and go, and the city's links with slavery gave the city links with many parts of the world. Being close to Ireland meant many new words were introduced to the dialect from that direction.

Recent changes in dialects are demonstrated by considering how a variant of Scouse can now be heard in North Wales. As people move and cities grow, the accent of a place will be influenced.

Language

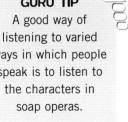
GURU TIP
A good way of listening to varied ways in which people speak is to listen to the characters in soap operas.

Words of passage
Here is a selection of some of the words English has borrowed from other languages (not including Latin, Greek, French and other Western European languages).

GURU TV
Find out how accent can be important in Literature, too, in the TV programmes.

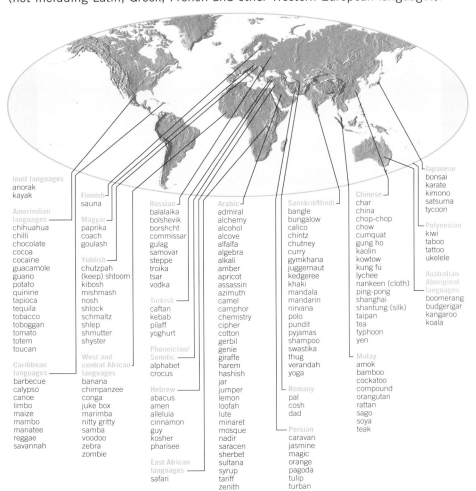

Inuit languages
anorak
kayak

Amerindian languages
chihuahua
chilli
chocolate
cocoa
cocaine
guacamole
guano
potato
quinine
tapioca
tequila
tobacco
toboggan
tomato
totem
toucan

Caribbean languages
barbecue
calypso
canoe
limbo
maize
mambo
manatee
reggae
savannah

Finnish
sauna

Magyar
paprika
coach
goulash

Yiddish
chutzpah
(keep) shtoom
kibosh
mishmash
nosh
shlock
schmaltz
shlep
shmutter
shyster

West and central African languages
banana
chimpanzee
conga
juke box
marimba
nitty gritty
samba
voodoo
zebra
zombie

East African languages
safari

Russian
balalaika
bolshevik
borshcht
commissar
gulag
samovar
steppe
troika
tsar
vodka

Turkish
caftan
kebab
pilaff
yoghurt

Phoenician/Semitic
alphabet
crocus

Hebrew
abacus
amen
alleluia
cinnamon
guy
kosher
pharisee

Arabic
admiral
alchemy
alcohol
alcove
alfalfa
algebra
alkali
amber
apricot
assassin
azimuth
camel
camphor
chemistry
cipher
cotton
gerbil
genie
giraffe
harem
hashish
jar
jumper
lemon
loofah
lute
minaret
mosque
nadir
saracen
sherbet
sultana
syrup
tariff
zenith
zero

Sanskrit/Hindi
bangle
bungalow
calico
chintz
chutney
curry
gymkhana
juggernaut
kedgeree
khaki
mandala
mandarin
nirvana
polo
pundit
pyjamas
shampoo
swastika
thug
verandah
yoga

Romany
pal
cosh
dad

Persian
caravan
jasmine
magic
orange
pagoda
tulip
turban
van

Chinese
char
china
chop-chop
chow
cumquat
gung ho
kaolin
kowtow
kung fu
lychee
nankeen (cloth)
ping-pong
shanghai
shantung (silk)
taipan
tea
typhoon
yen

Malay
amok
bamboo
cockatoo
compound
orangutan
rattan
sago
soya
teak

Japanese
bonsai
karate
kimono
satsuma
tycoon

Polynesian
kiwi
taboo
tattoo
ukelele

Australian Aboriginal languages
boomerang
budgerigar
kangaroo
koala

Spend a few minutes looking at the list of words above. You will probably recognize most of them, but may be surprised to notice the range of words that the English language has taken from other languages. Over time, these word borrowings have become part of our vocabulary and have made a 'passage' into everyday language.

Language and new technologies

One fascinating area of language change is the impact of new technologies. It is particularly interesting because the differences between spoken and written language are becoming blurred. You probably spend some of your time communicating via the Internet and everyone will rely on new technology more in the future.

This section takes a closer look at specific developments in online language. At the end of the section, you can practise by looking more closely at a website of the music events genre.

New media technologies such as the Internet combine images, text and sound. The function of language in Internet pages is often merely to complement the images and emphasise various links within the document. Conventions of website construction, such as the use of icons, have developed to help readers to navigate their way around the material.

As a result of the development of the Internet and electronic communication, exclusively online language has developed. The distinctions between written and spoken language are becoming blurred. On e-mail, people often write as if they were having a conversation and the more formal conventions of written English are breaking down. So-called 'net lingo' has now become so popular that many of the central or core terms in online language are familiar to a wide audience.

The following are examples of the acronyms which have developed through electronic communication and which are gradually being integrated in to our everyday language

- ISP - Internet service provider
- WAP - Wireless application protocol
- WYSIWYG (pronounced wizzywig) – what you see is what you get
- CD ROM – Compact disc read only memory

Internet hieroglyphics: Smileys

An example of the way in which Internet language is developing its own distinct set of codes and conventions is the development of what are called Smileys.

Smileys, or 'emoticons' are a set of symbols which have evolved to indicate emotions or feelings on screen. They often mimic facial expressions. The original Smiley symbol is a colon followed by a hyphen and a close bracket mark

: -)

If you turn the page clockwise so the left edge is at the top, the combination of symbols looks like a smiling face.

The symbol above is the basic Smiley which you will see most often, but there are many more and they provide an example of the way in which electronic interaction can alter the way you communicate information.

: - (I'm sad

: - \   I'm undecided

8 -   I wear glasses

: - 7   I'm being wry

GURU TIP
Electronic communication is communicating by computers, mobile phones and digital technologies.

GURU WEBSITE/TV
Find out more about the impact of new technology by looking at the AS Guru™ TV programmes and the website:
www.bbc.co.uk/asguru/english

As Smileys become more common, people are now using what are being termed non-Smileys, which are also symbols, which are being used to create meaning in an electronic text. Below are a number of examples.

<g>   Grinning, smiling

<l>   Laughing

<jk>   Just kidding

<lol>   Laughing out loud

<ty>   Thank you

<brb>   Be right back

You can see Smileys as an easy way to convey meaning when communicating online. They have originated in the same way that slang originates: they are a shorthand means of communicating with like-minded people. However, how will the use of such symbols affect language in the long run?

Text message 'slang'

Increasingly, people communicate with each other by electronic means. A good example of this is the growing use of text messaging on mobile phones. As context and the process of social interaction affect the language used to communicate ideas, thoughts and feelings, you can see how an understanding of pragmatics (see page 100) is becoming even more useful in the study of language.

For speed, new ways of communicating have developed which may seem unfamiliar to those people who do not use mobile phones or electronic mail. For instance, 'see you tomorrow' may be transcribed as 'c u 2morrow'. This reflects the need to use shorter words for technological reasons, for example, to reduce the amount of data to save space on the mobile phone's memory card. Text messaging can also be seen as reflecting a cultural shift towards people being more comfortable with the use of new technology.

The informal nature of text messages and their use of symbols is simply an example of how language develops. The meaning of the words has not altered, but the context in which they communicate has changed. The shortening of words is a key feature of text messaging. For instance:

'the' = 'da',   'that' = 'dat',   'enough' = 'enuff',   'about' = 'bout'.

Look at the following text messages and see if you can translate them:

Ru comin 2 nite?

CU L8r

Hiya, wot u up to ?

UR gr8

GURU TIP
Advertising is now common on mobile phones – see the next section on the language of advertising.

GURU TIP
Text messaging: the word 'messaging' has now entered the English language to mean the sending and receiving of mobile phone messages.

Language

The language of advertising

GURU WEBSITE
Look at the example of an advertisement on the AS Guru™ website and decide which audience it's aimed at:
www.bbc.co.uk/asguru/english

The language of advertising is a language of persuasion. When you look at a print-based advertisement in a newspaper or magazine you can usually identify its purpose by the specific vocabulary that's used.

Advertisements are made up of the following elements:

- layout
- language
- relationship between text and image

Layout is concerned with:

- Visuals: images and photographs
- Copy: the written text
- Graphics: lettering, size of font and the variety and different styles of typeface used.

When you look at the layout used in advertising, ask yourself:

- How does the image used in the advertisement fit in with the overall design of the advert?
- Where has the image been placed in relation to the rest of the advert?
- How much space has been given to the photograph or image that has been used?

Grammar in advertisements

To look at the grammar used in the language of advertising, it's important to recognise that this form of persuasive communication is encoded has specific connotations.

- Advertisers use sentence forms that you would be more used to seeing in spoken language. This is done to create an impression of familiarity between the reader and the advertiser.

- The use of imperatives is common in speech, but it's not used very often in writing, other than to give instructions, such as on official forms. However, imperatives are often used in advertising. For example:

| **'Buy today, don't delay!'** | **'Write now to claim your free gift'** |

- Have you noticed how newspaper reports in tabloid newspapers are often presented so that a paragraph contains only one sentence? This use of short paragraphs and of breaking text down into short sentences or phases is also popular in the language of advertising.

- Instead of using formal language, the advertiser will use colloquial language, that's the kind of language that you might use in everyday conversations. This creates a more informal and familiar tone. You might find a humorous or conversational tone, a direct address to the reader, and the use of first person plural pronouns like 'us' and 'we' to create an impression of friendliness and shared expectations and needs.

- In order to attract the attention of the reader and to ensure that the language, and therefore the message, of the advertiser is memorable, sound patterning devices are often used. You may be familiar with these terms from the study of poetry, but they are also used to great effect in the language of advertising. The most commonly used devices are:

- **Alliteration**
- **Assonance**
- **Onomatopoeia**
- **Rhyme**

The relationship between text and image

When you have looked at the layout of an advert and the language of the text, you will need to look more closely at the relationship between text and image.

- Look at the copy or the text used in the advert. What is the main message?

- What kind of language is being used to get the message across and does the image help to reiterate this message?

Look closely at the following advert. It is not for a product, but was produced for an anti-war campaign. Look at:

- layout
- language
- the relationship between image and text.

Language

GURU TIP

When you look at the anti-war advertisement, here are some things to think about.

How much space does the picture take up? What does the picture show – what impact would it have?

Look at the size of the text, how much there is of it and where it is placed.

What do the words say – what connotations do the words have?

This advert is an excellent example of the way in which the language and image are used to persuade the reader – not to buy, in this case, but to support the cause.

Audience profiling

A huge amount of money is spent on advertising and a lot of research goes into audience profiling – deciding exactly who the audience is, their tastes, their social situation and lifestyle. An audience profile is useful because it helps the creators of an advertisement to make decisions on the language to use.

Here are some features to consider when trying to determine an audience profile.

- Age
- Social class
- Gender
- Ethnicity and cultural diversity
- Geography and location

Different profiles foreground different aspects of the audience, depending on the needs of the profiler. Language will be chosen to fit the audience appropriately.

The language of literature

GURU TIP

Look at the pages on Spoken language for more on how people communicate through talking.

GURU TIP

Think about what Hopkins and Hardy may have been wanting you to feel about the views they describe in the two quotes on the right.

What is it that distinguishes the language of everyday speech or writing from the language of literature? Usually, people use language in a very unliterary way – even if what they are talking about is 'literary'. In conversation, you might describe a view as simply 'beautiful' or 'lovely', but a poet or writer would probably express it very differently. Authors don't know their audience and can't rely on gesture, tone of voice and other 'shorthand' means of communication: all they have are words on a page. Gerard Manley Hopkins, in his poem, 'Pied Beauty', wrote of a view as a

> Landscape plotted and pieced – fold, fallow and plough

and Thomas Hardy's 'The Melancholy Hussar of the German Legion' begins,

> Here stretch the downs; high and breezy and green.

Language in literature has to work a lot harder than the words of casual chatter. It has to paint pictures, and also convey the emotions the writer wants readers to feel.

Let's look at two poems to see how hard the language has to 'work' to help you see and feel as the poets intend. One poem is by Shakespeare and is about 400 years old. The other was written only a few years ago, so you can also examine how the language of literature changes. They both have the same theme – love.

Sonnet XVIII

Shall I compare thee to a summer's day?
Thou art more lovely and more temperate.
Rough winds so shake the darling buds of May,
And summer's lease hath all too short a date:
Sometime too hot the eye of heaven shines,
And often is his gold complexion dimm'd;
And every fair from fair sometime declines,
By chance, or nature's changing course, untrimm'd;
But thy eternal summer shall not fade,
Nor lose possession of that fair thou ow'st;
Nor shall Death brag thou wander'st in his shade,
When in eternal lines to time thou grow'st.
So long as men can breathe, or eyes can see,
So long lives this, and this gives life to thee.

William Shakespeare

Valentine

Not a red rose or a satin heart.

I give you an onion.
It is a moon wrapped in brown paper.
It promises light
like the careful undressing of love.

Here.
It will blind you with tears
like a lover.
It will make your reflection
a wobbling photo of grief.

I am trying to be truthful.

Not a cute card or a kissogram.

I give you an onion.
Its fierce kiss will stay on your lips,
possessive and faithful
as we are,
for as long as we are.

Take it.
Its platinum loops shrink to a wedding ring,
if you like.
Lethal.
Its scent will cling to your fingers,
cling to your knife.

Carol Ann Duffy

Now reread the poems and try to think about the similarities and differences in the ways that the poems have been written.

Lexis

- Shakespeare's poem uses the affectionate archaic form of you, 'thou', which indicates immediately how he feels towards his subject.

- It contains some vocabulary which you don't often hear now. Words like temperate have slightly altered in meaning since his day, but do not prevent you getting the gist of the poem.

- You can tell that the language is self-consciously formal, in honour of the woman he's writing to.

- Duffy is more down to earth – an onion is the most everyday vegetable! She includes several words which anchor her poem in the late 20th Century, such as satin heart, photo and kissogram. These words also give clues as to how she feels about her lover. You get the sense that she won't send a satin heart as it is tacky and too ordinary, and a kissogram is an equally unimaginative gift.

So, when you look at a literary text, consider whether the language is a) archaic or modern and b) formal or informal, and what that might tell you about it.

GURU TIP
The Lexis is the stock of words that a writer has to choose from.

Writing

Form

Shakespeare's poem is a sonnet, a form traditionally associated with love poetry. He sets up his comparison of the woman to a summer's day in the first eight lines (the octet) and then cleverly argues how she is, in fact, far lovelier in the remaining six (sestet). Read more about sonnets on pages 52–53.

Duffy writes in free verse. This allows her to give special emphasis to key ideas. Look how the one-line stanzas stand out from the rest of the poem on the page. Look at the one-word lines, Here and Lethal. What impact does their isolation have?

GURU TIP
See the Poetic form section of this book for more information.

See the Glossary of literary terms for definitions of a sonnet and free verse.

Ideas

Shakespeare has decided that the best way he can convey his feelings for his lover is to compare her – favourably – to something that most people would consider beautiful, a summer's day. He carefully sets out all the reasons why his lover triumphs in comparison, so his poem is a cleverly-argued extended metaphor. The metaphor is heightened, using superlatives, to express his heightened emotions.

Duffy also uses an extended metaphor as she explains why an onion is the perfect Valentine's gift. The poem is a series of justifications for her choice. Each stanza puts forward one reason why an onion best represents her feelings. In contrast to Shakespeare, Duffy's choice of image is downbeat, dealing in the mundane.

GURU TIP
See pages 42-43 for more on Metaphor.

The ending

Shakespeare concludes with a rhyming couplet and leaves the reader in no doubt of his feelings. The two last lines round off the 'argument' of the poem triumphantly and the final rhyme on 'see' and 'thee' ends the poem on a soft yet confident note.

Duffy's poem ends quite differently. The mood is not at all certain. There is even perhaps a threat implied. The onion's scent will cling to her lover's fingers and to a knife. Is there, perhaps, a potential for violence in their relationship? Or, is she simply highlighting the power of an onion's scent and emphasising how suitable it is as a Valentine's gift – an onion sticks to a knife as a lover sticks to a lover?

GURU TIP
In your wider reading, you could explore whether it is characteristic of contemporary literature to use everyday imagery. Do modern writers seem to suspect as false anything too rich or overstated?

Practice

Task 1

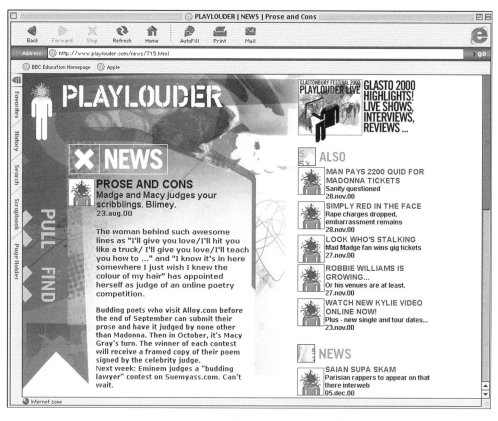

KEY SKILLS C3.1b

Look at the above page of an Internet site, then try to answer the questions below.

Look at the Guidance below if you need some help.

1. What can you learn from the language of this text?

2. How does this text differ from a text on a printed page?

3. Analyse this web page and assess its:

   - target audience
   - purpose

4. Then consider the visuals:

   - visual impact of the text
   - layout and design

5. Now assess the language:

- effect of short paragraphs

- language which helps to identify the writing as online language

- effect of using puns to introduce the article on the singer Macy Gray.

Guidance

1. The name alone (playlouder), a compound word, suggests a youthful, strong-willed approach to the subject matter.

2. Internet sites, like music videos, use graphics and sound to help create meaning - not text alone.

- Paragraphs are generally shorter than in prose texts. This is due in part to the layout of particular web pages, but also because of the rapid way you read information from a screen.

- The narrative structure is not linear, as it would be in a prose text: there is no beginning, middle and end. Instead, the way in which the text is put together is called an 'alternative structure'.

- typeface, paragraphing and use of images (do the photographs and images relate to the text?)

Task 2

Record a five-minute segment of a television quiz show. What do you notice about the way in which a chosen contestant interacts with the programme's host?

- What is the mode of address?
- Is the register used formal or informal?
- Are the intonation and pace important?
- What is the tone of the contestant's responses?
- Does either person have an interesting accent or dialect?

Now listen to a speech-based radio programme which includes an interview, such as a magazine programme on Radio 4. What do you notice about the way in which the interviewee interacts with the interviewer?

- What is the mode of address?
- Is the register used formal or informal?
- Are the intonation and pace important?
- What is the tone of the interviewee's responses?
- Does either person have an interesting accent or dialect?

Comment on the differences and similarities between the two conversations.

KEY SKILL
By doing a similar task you will be doing the following activities: 'read and synthesise information from two extended documents about a complex subject' which is **Key Skill C3.2**.

Task 3

Listen to an extract from a stand-up comedy sketch. Choose a live routine, if you can, as this will allow you to hear material which is being presented to an audience.

- What do you notice about the register of the comedian?
- How spontaneous is the speech?
- Has the material been scripted or do you think that the comedian is using ad lib to aid the delivery of the show's content?

KEY SKILL
Discussing a task like this in class could help you get **Key Skill C3.1a** because you will be 'contributing to a group discussion about a complex subject'.

Practice

The material is taken from a pack called '6 Billion and One' and was compiled as part of a project run by the United Nations Population fund. Two British charities , which work in the area of reproductive health were involved in the project, which aimed to make young people aware of important issues connected with population growth.

The pack was sponsored in order to encourage people to participate more fully and raise awareness of an important issue. By using the singer Geri Halliwell, the message would have the potential of reaching a wider audience. Fifteen to eighteen year-olds were given the task of writing a letter to the Prime Minister, Tony Blair, about how the UK Government is dealing with the issue of population growth.

The language in the text has been used in order to convey a complex set of messages and to ensure that the political message of the text is understood. In its current format its purpose is to inform.

Read the text closely, then try the task given on the next page.

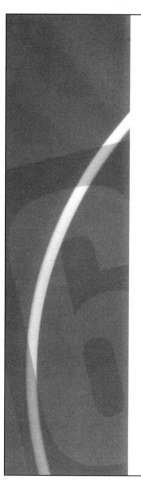

An Introduction by GERI HALLIWELL

a single voice can make a world of difference

United Nations Population Fund Goodwill Ambassador for the *face to face* campaign

Welcome to 6 Billion And One

I was deeply honoured to be offered the chance to become a United Nations Population Fund Goodwill Ambassador.

As my first official assignment, I'm delighted to be lending my face to the United Nations Population Fund's *face to face* campaign. It's my role to turn the spotlight on the struggles faced by women in developing countries, who have no access to contraception, no protection against AIDS and are at serious risk of losing their lives every time they have a baby.

The issues are important, as 1999 will see the world's population hitting six billion people for

asking him to commit his Government to working with the international community to bring about change while there's still a chance.

The next few years are critical. What happens now will have a profound effect on the world you, and your children, inherit in the future. Every competition entry will be delivered to Number 10 Downing Street, so your voice truly can make a world of difference.

I hope you'll read the **Six Billion And One** pack and get your entry form in to your teacher – the prize is a trip to Kenya for you, your teacher and a friend or parent.

When you have done this, practise writing for the same audience, but for a different type of medium. For example, you could write a three minute script as part of a speech-based radio programme. Remember that writing for an audience who can only hear what is being said and cannot rely on visual images and prompts is a distinct skill.

As well as the genre and audience, you will need to think about:
- the angle – what will be the focus of your script?
- the purpose – will your script inform, educate or entertain?

Your script will need to contain information about:
- Geri Halliwell's role as Goodwill Ambassador.
- The issue of population growth.
- Why your listeners would want to write.

Language

Key points about language

Language
- Language is used to communicate ideas, thoughts and emotions.

Audience and purpose
- Writers need to know who their writing is for in order to make decisions about language.
- All texts have a purpose – something they aim to do.

Grammar
- The study of the component parts of language and how they fit together.
- The rules of grammar help the author to communicate his or her intentions.

Semantics
- The study of the meaning of words.
- Semantic fields
- **synonyms**, **antonyms** and **hyponyms**
- **collocation**

Phonology and pragmatics
- **Phonetics** is the study of sounds made by the human voice.
- The study of decoding meaning and the social conventions of language involves **pragmatics**.

Spoken language
- When studying spoken language you need to look at mode of address, register, intonation, tone, accent and **dialect**.

Language and new technologies
- New technologies have had a formidable impact on the language people use.
- The Internet combines images, text and sound and is heavily iconographic.
- Text messaging is reliant on truncated words and the use of symbols.

The language of advertising
- Advertising uses language to persuade.
- The relationship between image and text is what makes an effective advertisement.

Assessment Objectives

The Assessment Objectives for Literature are:

AO1   you must write well and in a knowledgeable way

AO2   you must respond with knowledge and understanding to the play, having informed and considered ideas about it.

AO3   you must assess the way Shakespeare's choice of form, structure and language shapes meanings.

AO4   you must have independent opinions and judgements informed by different interpretations of literary texts by other readers. So, have your own readings of the play(s) but be aware of the readings of other people, such as fellow students, teachers and critics.

AO5   you must show understanding of the contexts in which literary texts are written and understood. Context is a complex issue but is not something you should be frightened of. It might sound like a new idea to you, but you have been dealing with issues of context during all of the time you were studying Shakespeare for SATs and GCSE. Whenever you think about different readings, or language, or form you are analysing one of the contexts of the text.

The Assessment Objectives for Language are:

AO1:   you must communicate clearly the knowledge, understanding and insight appropriate to the study of language, using appropriate terminology and accurate and coherent written expression.

AO4:   you must understand, discuss and explore concepts and issues relating to language in use.

The Assessment Objectives that apply to original writing are:

AO1:   communicate clearly the knowledge, understanding and insight appropriate to the study of language, using appropriate terminology and accurate, coherent written expression.

AO2:   demonstrate expertise and accuracy in writing for a variety of specific purposes and audiences, drawing on knowledge of linguistic features to explain and comment on choices made.

AO4:   understand, discuss and explore concepts and issues relating to language in use.

The Assessment Objectives for Language and Literature are:

- communicate clearly and accurately, using appropriate terminology
- distinguish, describe and interpret variation on meaning and form
- respond to texts using literary and linguistic concepts and approaches
- understand the importance of context in changing meaning
- identify how attitudes and values are conveyed in speech and writing
- show you are aware of audience and purpose in your writing

Preparing for the coursework

Preparing for your coursework is an important part of your exam. Your coursework folder will be marked by more than one person, so you can be sure that all students will be treated in the same way and the mark will be a fair reflection of your ability.

This is the section of the exam over which you will have the greatest control and where you have the best chance to demonstrate your strengths. The mark you get for this could be important in raising your overall grade. You have plenty of time for planning, drafting and revising, so use it wisely.

The coursework gives you the opportunity to demonstrate wider reading and your ability to make connections between texts. Think carefully about complementary texts. The texts you read for the coursework won't be read in class in as much detail as the Set Texts. Make sure you keep up with the reading in your own time.

Literature coursework: what you should do

- Read through your texts with care.
- Select your question carefully to reflect the areas that most interest you in the text.
- Read widely from a selection of other texts by your chosen author, critical writing about the book or author, and any other sources which seem appropriate.
- Make notes as you read and keep them in an ordered way.
- Make use of helpful quotations from other texts if you find them relevant, but make sure you indicate where they come from and whose ideas they are.
- Keep a list of all the books you've read so that you can include a bibliography at the end of the essay.
- Plan your essay.
- Follow the rules of writing a critical essay (page 78).
- Discuss your plan with your teacher, if possible.
- Give yourself plenty of time to draft and redraft your work.
- Hand in your first draft so your teacher can comment on it.
- Aim to improve your essay in subsequent drafts.
- Be meticulous about deadlines. This is an exam. You could be penalised for not handing in an essay on time.
- Be sure that you have covered the range of work required for a coursework folder.
- Be sure that the essays cover a range of topics which demonstrate your ability to discuss a variety of literary issues.

Literature coursework: what you should <u>not</u> do

- Don't try to write an essay without reading a text right through. You can't write an essay on a text just by knowing a summary of it.

- Don't try to write an essay without first making notes on the text. However good your memory, it will save you time and trouble to have all your evidence ready to hand before writing.

- Don't wait until the last minute to start your work. You're given a longer period of time to complete this essay for the good reason that this is an extended essay which should demonstrate wider reading. It's meant to take time.

- Don't hope for an extension to complete your essay. It's an exam and you're expected to hand it in on time.

- Don't try and pass off someone else's ideas as your own. You should incorporate the ideas into your own thinking and use your own words. It's perfectly acceptable to use critical writing to inform your work, but if you're using the exact wording, be sure to indicate what you've used and the sources from which it came. Examiners are familiar with critical writing and they will notice when it's not your own work.

Language and literature coursework

For AS Language and Literature coursework you're required to write for different audiences and purposes. You'll have a wide variety of examples to choose from. Your choice will affect the style of writing that you select. For instance, you could:

- Write to entertain
A short story
A stand up comedy routine
A radio script

- Write to persuade
A piece of text for an advertising campaign
A moral fable

- Write to inform
A press release
A newspaper article

Before you set about writing for an audience, revise what you have learnt in class.

Exemplar essays

Very often, students have a general feeling that goes something like this:

'Well, I know all the rules, but how do I put these into an essay?'

There are quite a few things you can do to help yourself, and several ways in which your teacher will be able to help you. One of the best ways to learn is from other students.

- Are there a few friends in your class with whom you could exchange essays?
- Are there any essays done by past students at your school or college that you could read?

If the answer to either or both of these questions is yes, here's what you could do.

- Ask your teacher if you might have a copy of the Assessment Objectives specific to the Exam Syllabus which you are following.
- Ask for a copy of the marking criteria that the board sends to teachers so that they can all mark to the same standard.

Sometimes schools and colleges are unable to afford individual copies for all students, but you could offer to pay for them to be copied. It will be money well spent.

When you have these, you can look at the essays you have between you and compare them to the criteria which you are supposed to meet.

- What criteria/objectives have been met by the essays in front of you?
- What more could have been added to improve the mark?

It's not always necessary to look at the essays of the best students, although this can help you to see how they structure and present their work. You can learn not only from what has been put in, but also from recognising what might have been left out. Provided your discussions about the essays are constructive and mature, the positive 'criticism' will benefit everyone involved. It will help you to be more critical with your own essays.

AS Guru™ English

In this book, you'll find that you've been given a handy summary of the Assessment Objectives (page 117) that gives you an idea of what is common to all the boards. There are also two essays for you to look at, an example of a coursework essay and an essay done under exam conditions, in forty-five minutes.

They are both good examples of work, but by no means perfect. Remember, there are many ways of writing an essay and the teacher will judge each one on it's own merits. Each paragraph of the exemplar essays contains teacher comments in **bold** to help you assess the essays, and where an Assessment Objective has been met, it's highlighted by an asterisk (*) and the wording of the objective is maintained.

Coursework essay

This has been done over a period of time. You can really influence your grade by using your time wisely in this section. Make use of all your opportunities to draft and discuss your essay before you hand in the final version to be marked. You're not under pressure of time, and it's expected that the work you hand in will reflect this in the care and attention shown to structure and proofreading (your grammar, spelling and syntax should receive your closest attention); in gaining a thorough knowledge of the texts through close reading; and showing evidence of wider reading. In the example provided in this book, the student has, in many ways, written an excellent essay. The teacher comment indicates what more the student could have done to improve his overall mark.

Question:

Examine the way in which Bram Stoker's *Dracula* and Oscar Wilde's *The Picture of Dorian Gray* deal with notions of sexuality and desire.

Answer:

The contemporary audience of these novels would not have tolerated literature dealing explicitly with ideas of sex and sexuality; nevertheless, both can be seen as highly sexual texts. Indeed, passages from *The Picture of Dorian Gray* were used as evidence at the trial of Oscar Wilde for homosexuality. However, whilst Wilde's novel relies mainly on subtle inference and implication, Dracula has a strong and highly charged sexual subtext which permeates the novel.

Teacher comment: This is a good opening paragraph which directly addresses the question without actually repeating the wording of the title. The student has indicated what are the key similarities and differences in the two texts. At the same time, he directs your attention to the *context* in which the ideas should be seen, by referring to the 'contemporary audience' of the two novels and the *attitudes and values* which would have shaped the *interpretation* of the text. The second paragraph moves swiftly to develop these points.

One of the key similarities between the two texts is the obvious seductiveness and sexual magnetism of the eponymous characters. In Dorian's case this is due to his appearance, whereas for Dracula, it is in spite of it. **(The student offers an opinion, then supports it with short, integrated quotations from the texts.)** As Basil Hallward says, Dorian is 'made to be worshipped', in stark contrast to Dracula's 'hideous' face of 'extraordinary pallor'. Both the portrait and Lord Henry help change Dorian from the 'simple' and 'innocent' boy that Hallward knew to the 'hideous' face of his soul recorded on the canvas. As he looks at the portrait for the first time, 'The sense of his own beauty came on him like a revelation.' He realises the power and opportunities which his attractiveness will give him. **(Quotation is followed by analysis.)** Despite the fact that he will 'plough the depths of degradation', he will always have a 'pure, sweet, innocent face' and this is part of his allure. He is adored by women everywhere – even to the point of saying 'I am sick of women who love one.' He seems to have the same effect on men, although this is slightly more ambiguous. The 'rough' assistant to the frame maker regards Dorian with 'a look of shy wonder.' 'He had never seen anyone so marvellous.' His first effects on both Basil and Henry are also intriguing – Basil is 'dominated soul, brain, and power' by Dorian, whereas Lord Henry looks at him with 'dreamy, languorous eyes.' **(The student does not lose sight of the fact that this is a comparative essay. He moves on to comment on the central character of the second text, continuing to compare and contrast.)** There is something a little more sinister about the desire which Dracula evokes in women. A literal reading of the text would suggest that an 'encounter' with a vampire is a violent and unpleasant attack on the 'victim'. However, a closer look at the subtext allows for a sexual reading, whereby the experience is enjoyable and erotic, albeit tinged with retrospective guilt and shame. **(Here the student demonstrates an understanding that there can be more than one meaning/reading of the text.)** The clearest account of Dracula's power and potency come in his 'nocturnal encounter' with Mina. It is important to note that the vampire cannot enter a new room without first being invited in – this is an extraordinary testament to his allure – even Mina, who knows first hand of Jonathan's horrendous experience in Castle Dracula, is seduced into inviting him in.

Teacher comment: In this second paragraph the student has developed the themes of sexuality and desire in terms of the 'appearance' of the characters and their sexual magnetism. In subsequent paragraphs, he continues by discussing the coded presentation of sexual orientation, gender and sexual identity, the representation of female characters and traditional notions of love, all of which could be said to be possible themes in the text. He organises his ideas thematically, developing them in carefully structured paragraphs. You can see clearly how he follows the pattern of presenting a point of view, supporting it with evidence and then analysing the evidence to demonstrate how it works to make meaning in the text. He begins the paragraph with a reference to 'seductiveness' and ends with the 'seduced' victim.

A feature of the sexual subtext in Dracula is its frequent perversity, and horrific sexual imagery, which simply isn't present in Wilde's novel. Almost every contemporary sexual taboo is violated or threatened by the vampire. The vampiric act, whilst being pseudo-sexual, is by no means free of horror, and seeks to blur the boundaries between pleasure and pain, or perhaps destroy them. Harker's encounter in the castle contrasts his 'deadly fear' with 'languorous ecstasy'; her breath is 'honey sweet', yet has a 'bitter offensiveness'. Vampirism inverts the sanctity of both monogamy, and more horrifically, motherhood – the vampire women feed on the 'half-smothered child'. The vampire threatens what the novel sees as perhaps the principal function of women – Harker chauvinistically claims that after she had lost her child, the wailing mother was 'better dead'. **(Here the student discusses not only the themes of Gender Representation, Sexual Taboo and the challenge they represent to the reader, but also refers indirectly to the generic presentation of 'horror' in the text.)**

What the authors are trying to achieve by the use of such extensive sexual undercoding is often as ambiguous as the passages themselves. In Wilde's novel, it is easy to look upon Lord Henry as the voice of the author, and see the key message as an advocation of hedonism... ... A closer examination of the text reveals this to be slightly tenuous however. Wilde frequently seems to consciously undermine Lord Henry; many of the statements he makes are proved false by the book – 'It is not in you, Dorian, to commit a murder.' is just one example of this...

... Although, as with much of the sexual undercurrent in Dracula, it is impossible to tell whether this is the reading which Stoker intended or merely an accident of his subconscious. In this case however, the sexual reading seems so transparently overt that it is difficult to see it as anything other than a conscious choice of the author.) This scene is part of an overtly 'moral' undercurrent, simply not present in such an explicit form in The Picture of Dorian Gray, which suggests that polygamous women, or those who are sexually active, are evil and will be punished

Teacher comment: These two paragraphs are not reproduced in their entirety, but it is possible to see how the student has referred to what he sees to be the author's intent in presenting certain scenes and themes. While he offers an opinion on how he reads the underlying messages of the texts, he acknowledges that there might be other readings.

Concluding paragraph:

Both texts then, are strongly charged with notions of sex and desire, *Dracula* could perhaps even be described as primarily a sexual novel. In some cases these ideas are deeply undercoded and may not be apparent on a first reading, in other cases, such as the final death of Lucy in *Dracula*, they are lucid. Yet for both texts, the sexual subtext acts as one of the means to the end of what is actually a traditionalist moral stance. A close examination of *The Picture of Dorian Gray* reveals that what is ostensibly an excited advocation of Dorian's form of aesthetic decadence is actually a savage indictment of it. Although the sexual overtones of Vampirism give it a kind of grotesque allure, the final reconciliation of *Dracula* suggests the triumph of Christianity over Satanism, of West over East, and more subtly, of men over women. It propounds a ferocious condemnation of promiscuous women, and portrays sexual awakening, especially in females, as depraved and even evil. Both Wilde and Stoker use erotic undercoding to enhance, rather than subvert, the conservative moral stances which they are advocating.

Teacher comment: This is a good conclusion which weighs up all the evidence gathered in the essay about the two texts and gives a personal response to these. While the essay has been careful throughout to acknowledge alternative readings, here the student has decided to present an overview of his own. The essay as a whole is clearly structured, closely argued and supported with evidence from the texts. The student has used the extended period of time allowed for coursework to present work of very high quality, which shows evidence of careful planning, wide reading, and above all, a thorough knowledge of the texts. He has met many of the Assessment Objectives, interpreting *variation in meaning and form*, *an awareness of how context might shape meaning* and *how attitudes and values are created and conveyed*. However, as a student of English Language and Literature, although his essay has referred to the way in which language creates meaning, he has not clearly signposted the way in which *insights are gained from <u>combined</u> literary and linguistic study*. Nor has this student included a bibliography which indicates what books/materials he has used in his wider reading. Consequently, he would not have received the very top mark.

Exam essay

The example you have for this essay on Mary Shelley's *Frankenstein* was done in exam conditions in forty-five minutes in the student's own handwriting. The spelling, punctuation and expressions used have been left exactly as they were written down. The exam was done as an Open Text exam, where the student was able to use her own copy of the text. Again, this is a very sound essay but the pressure of working in timed conditions is reflected in this essay. The teacher comment will guide you through the strengths and weaknesses of this essay.

Question:

Re-read Chapter IV. <u>What</u> is the <u>significance</u> of <u>this chapter</u> to the novel as <u>a whole</u> and <u>how</u> does it <u>affect your thoughts and feelings</u>?

Plan:

– significance? M Waldman becomes 'true friend' of Victor & encourages him to explore more /contrast with V's warning to W.(q. pg 45) V. imp stage in story-destroy/determined? Pt of no retrn.

– discards frnds, gets 'great esteem' at Uni-encourages his ego to get more.

Turns attntion to anatomy/life for 1st time-lnks with galvanism – 'became myself capable..'

'consummation (comm. Sexual lang) of my toils' 'began the creation' 'dabbled in the unhallowed (com religious lang)...'

– to whole?concern abt how to use power not if – hubris

Feelings? 1st feelings of criticism of Fr? Unsettling for reader?

Structural/Building up of tension

Teacher comment: Despite the pressure of time, the student has wisely made a brief plan. This helps her to structure the essay and to remember key quotes which she has assembled before starting the essay. She has underlined the key words in the title and used this as a guide. Finally, she has placed a single neat line through the plan so the examiner is aware that this is not part of the answer.

Answer:

Chapter IV of Frankenstein is the last chapter before Victor actually creates the creature 'on a dreary night of November', and as such acts partly to build up the atmosphere of tension and impending danger for the reader prior to the climactic event of The Creature's birth.

Teacher comment: The student begins, quite correctly, by addressing the question directly. However, she narrows the essay down to just one of the many elements she has identified as being significant. She would have done better to mention some of the other ways in which the Chapter is significant. This would have given a structure to her essay which she could have followed step by step.

This chapter begins highlighting how from the day M Waldman shows Frankenstein around his labratory **(sp.)** Victor's 'sole occupation' was natural philosophy, especially chemistry. The use of the word 'sole' in this context seems entirely appropriate, echoing Shelley's careful choice of highly suggestive language throughout the novel. Here we become aware of the isolating effect of the work in which Frankenstein is engaged, cut off from all human contact. As Victor states at the end of Chapter III 'thus ended a day memorable to me: it decided my future destiny'. Chapter IV can thus be viewed as a watershed, or point of no return in Victor's life. From hereon, he races headlong towards the 'summit', 'the most gratifying consummation' of his 'labour' and in hindsight, his doom. Again, the language suggests the way in which Frankenstein's work replaces human emotions and feelings. All his ardour and passion are diverted to his work rather than to his family or his betrothed, Elizabeth.

Teacher comment: In this paragraph, after a rather awkward start, the student gets into her stride. She is able to comment on the relation of this chapter to the whole text and to the specific development of character. The student is also able to demonstrate *insights gained from combined literary and linguistic study* by highlighting Shelley's choice of diction.

While Frankenstein seems to be actively discarding his real friends in favour of his studies, there is an interesting parallel which is developed between the relationship he forms with his professors, in particular M. Waldman, whom he describes as his 'true friend' (although in reality he is a more of a mentor), and Walton. Walton, in his letters home to his sister, declares that he has grown 'to love (Frankenstein) as a brother'. In turn, Frankenstein himself becomes the mentor. The contrast lies in the fact that while the professors appear to urge Victor, inadvertently perhaps, to dabble 'among the unhallowed damps of the grave', Victor in his turn is adamant that he will not pass on the knowledge which would lead to 'destruction and infallible misery'. He has learnt 'how dangerous is the acquirement of knowledge' to the man who 'aspires to become greater than his nature will allow'. With hindsight, Victor has recognised that the moment in his past, which is described in this chapter, was the pivotal one which led to his downfall. The biblical language used here, highlites **(sp.)** Shelley's theme of Hubris and the dangers of too much Scientific interference with nature and the works of God. The analogy with Adam and the Fall are present here as they are in the rest of the text. Here Shelley intends, perhaps that the reader should consider the duties of a 'real friend'.

Teacher comment: An over long and slightly muddled paragraph. The student is attempting to tackle a number of relevant issues, thematic, linguistic and moral. It might have worked more successfully if she had separated these into different paragraphs. However, she does make several valid points about the author's intentions and *how attitudes and values are created and conveyed*.

The Chapter describes Frankenstein's meteoric rise as a student. He notes with not a little self-satisfaction that his 'ardour' was the 'astonishment of the students' and his 'proficiency that of the masters', progressing to 'great esteem' and admiration. With all the evidence of his puffed up pride, there seems to be an ominus **(sp.)** amount of warning here that a 'fall' must surely follow.

Teacher comment: A good point, succinctly made.

The next pivotal point in this chapter is reached when Victor finally discovers the principle from which 'life proceed(s)'. The significance of this stage in the novel is clearly huge in that it underpins the progress of the narrative.

Teacher comment: Again, a good point but one that is not developed. There is no evidence given to support this statement or to explain in what way this chapter underpins the progress of the narrative. The student seems to assume that the examiner knows what she means. She needs to be specific.

The reader's attitudes towards Frankenstein alter considerably over the course of this chapter. From the interest and sympathy created by his interactions with Walton and the story of his early life, towards a greater feeling of awe at his work and then finally, to criticism of his actions and behaviour as he 'shunned (his) fellow creatures'. At times we are discomfited to hear of the 'irresistible **(sp.)** hold' of his work on his imagination, while his loved ones pine at home without any word from him. His desire to imprison himself in his 'workshop of filthy creation' seems incomprehensible when he could so easily have created new life by simply marrying and producing children with the patient and loving Elizabeth.

Teacher comment: Here the student has addressed how the reader responds to the narrative, but she fails to point out the craft of the writer in unsettling our notions of the hero. Since Walton initially presents Victor to us as heroic, we begin at this point to learn some less than pleasant facts about him. It prepares us for the later accusations of the Creature that Victor Frankenstein is vain and neglectful of his proper duties.

In this chapter, Victor's motives for his work are open to question. While he debates the 'manner in which (he) should employ' his new found knowledge, he never once questions whether he <u>should</u> use it. His disregard for the consequences of his action are echoed throughout the novel, and could be perceived by some readers as the destructive 'male' thirst for knowledge, power and god-like status. His claim that as a result of his creative powers, 'No father could claim the gratitude of his child so completely as I should deserve theirs', creates a feeling of distaste in the reader which remains throughout the rest of our reading.

Teacher comment: An attempt here by the student to acknowledge an alternative reading is not entirely successful. She does not explain why the thirst for knowledge should be seen as a 'male' attribute, nor does she offer an alternative reading. However, she ends the paragraph with a sound statement responding to the title.

This chapter is very significant to the wider structure of the novel in that it acts as a bridge between Victor's early life, and the unhappiness of his later life; the transition being charted in detail, building up tension to the climactic Chapter V and the Creature's Narrative.

Teacher comment: This is a weak conclusion since it does not really relate to the main points in the essay. They are valid points and as such would carry some marks, but a conclusion should build on what is discussed in the essay. Note that in the planning, the student has not made any notes on the Introduction or Conclusion. These are the two weakest points of the essay.

There are some strong moments in the essay where the student is fluent and clear about the points she is making. She covers a wide range of literary and linguistic objectives. However, sometimes expression is weak or clumsy and there are a few spelling mistakes, perhaps as a consequence of working in exam conditions. She would not be too severely penalised for this. Where she has followed her plan, the ideas are linked and the structure is smooth, but at times she moves rather abruptly from one point to the next. Nevertheless, this is a good essay overall, and would possibly be given a high B or a low A.

Glossary of literary terms

Allegory: writing in which the characters, events or locations represent other things, usually abstract ideas.

Alliteration: usually the repetition of initial consonant sounds in closely successive words.

Assonance: a repetition in the vowel sound but not in the consonant.

Ballad: a poem which narrates a story written in four line stanzas. Simple in structure, is is a form of poetry which has traditionally been used in the writing of songs (folk ballads) to accompany music. It makes use of repetition and refrains and simple rhymes.

Bathos: a technique used to add humour by changing tone suddenly from the sublime to the ridiculous.

Blank verse: unrhyming verse in iambic pentameter, as used by William Shakespeare.

Caesura: a short pause in the middle of a line of poetry.

Conceit: an image or an idea in which a metaphor is made more striking by the dissimilarity between the things being compared. The skill lies in drawing a connection between the subject of comparison and the thing to which it is being compared.

Couplet: two consecutive lines of verse which rhyme, and often have the same metre.

Didactic: writing which aims to teach or instruct.

Elegy: a poem with a theme of sorrow or mourning.

Elision: the striking out of an unstressed syllable in order to maintain the metre, e.g. o'er, and e'en.

End rhyme: a rhyme which falls at the end of a line.

Enjambment: when there is no pause or punctuation at the end of a line of poetry and the sense carries over on to the next line.

Epigram: a short, brief poem or verse which makes a witty or clever statement.

Euphemism: the substitution of a mild or inoffensive term to describe something which may be unpleasant or painful if described bluntly.

Eye rhyme or sight rhyme: end words of lines of verse which are spelled alike and so appear to rhyme visually but do not sound like each other, e.g. 'bough' and 'rough'.

Feminine rhyme: lines of poetry which end with an unstressed syllable. Conversely, lines which end with a stressed syllable are said to have Masculine Endings.

Free verse: verse which does not follow any traditional metre (regular stress patterns), rhyme or form.

Haiku: Poetic form of Japanese origin. It has three lines in which the first and third line contain five syllables while the second line has seven. It is concise and is generally used to convey vividly a philosophical or spiritual idea.

Heroic couplet: a pair of rhyming lines written in iambic pentameter and rhyming aa,bb,cc. It is the form used by Geoffrey Chaucer in The Canterbury Tales.

Hyperbole: a deliberate exaggeration or overstatement, used to add emphasis or humour or to express strong emotions, such as love or despair.

Iamb: a metrical foot of one unstressed syllable followed by a stressed syllable.

Iambic pentameter: A line of verse which contains five iambs (see Iamb above).

Imagery: images or pictures in the mind produced by language. The presentation of ideas and objects which may be associated in a writer's imagination with something else.

Internal rhyme: rhymes that occur within lines.

Irony: difficult to define because it's used by writers in a variety of forms and for a variety of purposes.

a) Verbal irony – saying one thing and meaning another

b) Dramatic irony – when a reader or audience perceives the significance of an event or situation of which a character or

characters may have limited knowledge.

c) The gap between hopes and dreams and the realistic truth of a situation.

Used to expose humorously human weaknesses such as pretence and hypocrisy, to criticise an idea or a situation, or to heighten tragedy and drama.

Lyric: originally used to describe a poem which was accompanied by music played on a lyre. Current use of the term refers to a short poem, divided into stanzas, which directly express the poet's own thoughts and feelings.

Metaphor: a figure of speech in which a comparison is made between two objects where the qualities of one are used to identify the other. While a simile stops at comparing two things, the metaphor goes further, it omits the 'like' and 'as' and identifies one thing as another.

Metre: the rhythm of the language in poetry which makes up a repeated pattern of stressed and unstressed syllables. Each unit is referred to as a foot.

Narrative: the story, or events in the order in which they actually took place.

Onomatopeia: when the sound of a word echoes the sense of it.

Oxymoron: putting together words which seem to contradict each other, as in 'bitter-sweet'.

Paradox: a statement which seems at first glance to be absurd or self-contradictory but gradually reveals that it contains a truth which it expresses in an original way. For example, the quotation from Macbeth 'Fair is foul and foul is fair'. This refers to things not always being what they seem.

Parody: exaggerated imitation of a serious piece of literature or a serious event to add humour or, sometimes, to make a serious point through the humour.

Pathos: writing which seeks to convey deep feelings which arouse pity or sorrow in the reader/audience without necessarily being sentimental.

Protagonist: the character, in a narrative, who is responsible for instigating and driving the action forward.

Ode: a long lyric poem. The style and subject are serious, and the language often elaborate.

Personification: giving inanimate objects human characteristics of thought and feelings.

Plot: the sequence of events in which a story is told in a text, which may be different to the order in which the events actually took place.

Rhetoric: the art of presenting an idea or a position expressively or persuasively.

Rhyme: created when the final syllables of two or more words have identical sound patterns.

Rhyme scheme: the repeated pattern of end-rhymes in a stanza.

Satire: the use of irony or exaggeration to highlight certain ideas and events, and impress on the reader/audience an awareness of a problem or situation.

Simile: a figure of speech in which two things are compared in order to produce a vivid image. The comparison is made directly with the words 'like' or 'as' used to link the two things.

Soliloquy: a dramatic monologue where a character speaks their thoughts out loud. Often to give the reader/audience an insight into the mind and psychology of a character.

Sonnet: a tight form of poetry which contains 14 lines and rhymes in accordance with one of various definite schemes, for example, Shakespearean and Petrarchan.

Stanza: the groups of lines into which a poem is divided. These are not always regular patterns. Some groupings of lines have specific names such as Couplets(two lines), or Tercets (three lines), Quatrains (four lines), Sestets (six lines), Septets (seven lines), and Octets or Octaves (eight lines).

Glossary of language terms

Abstract: abstract nouns denote feelings, ideas, qualities and things you cannot touch.

Active and passive: many verbs can be active or passive. For example, bite: The dog bit Ben. (active), Ben was bitten by the dog. (passive).

Adjective: an adjective is a word that describes somebody or something. Adjectives (and adverbs) can have comparative and superlative forms. The comparative form is adjective + -er (for one-syllable adjectives, and some two-syllable) or more + adjective (for adjectives of two or more syllables).

Adverb: adverbs give extra meaning to a verb, an adjective, another adverb or a whole sentence.

Affix: a morpheme which is not in itself a word, but is attached to a word. An affix can be a prefix (*in*tolerant, *dis*like) or a suffix (kind*ness*, play*ing*).

Antonym: a word with a meaning opposite to another.

Article: 'a', 'an' and 'the' are articles. 'A' (an before a vowel sound) is the indefinite article; 'the' is the definite article. Articles are a type of determiner.

Auxiliary verb: these are verbs that are used together with other verbs, for example, *we are going*.

Blend: the process of combining phonemes into larger elements, such as clusters, syllables and words. Also refers to a combination of two or more phonemes, particularly at the beginning and end of words, *st, str, nt, pl, nd*.

Clause: a clause is a group of words that expresses an event (*she drank some water*) or a situation (*she was thirsty/she wanted a drink*). It usually contains a subject (*she* in the examples) and verb (*drank/was/wanted*).

Collocation: this means putting two or more things together, referring to the in-built associations native speakers of a language apply to particular pairs of words, for example, salt and pepper.

Compound word: a word made up of two other words, for example, football.

Conjunction: a word used to link clauses within a sentence. For example, in the following sentence, *but* and *if* are conjunctions: *It was raining but it wasn't cold.*

Connotation: meaning which is implied in addition to the primary meaning.

Consonant: a speech sound in which breath is at least partially obstructed and, when combined with a vowel, forms a syllable.

Deixis/Deictic: pronoun references, such as **it**, **this** and **that,** which ensure that the listener knows what, where and to whom the language is referring.

Denotation: the dictionary definition of a word is known as its **denotation**. This is the clear, objective, unbiased meaning.

Dialect: a dialect is a variety of a language used in a particular area and which is distinguished by certain features of grammar or vocabulary.

Etymology: the study of the origin and history of words.

Genre: this term refers to different types of writing, each with its own specific characteristics, which relate to origin (legend/folk tale), or reader interest area – the types of books individuals particularly choose to read: adventure, romance, science fiction.

Lexis: the study of words and vocabulary.

Morpheme: the smallest unit of meaning.

Noun: a noun is a word that denotes somebody or something.

Phoneme: a phoneme is the smallest contrastive unit of sound in a word. There are approximately 44 phonemes in English (the number varies depending on the accent).

Pragmatics: the meanings which are dependent, not on the language alone, but on the setting in which it takes place.

Predicate: the predicate is that part of a sentence which is not the subject but which gives information about the subject. So, in the sentence *Clare went to school*, *'Clare'* is the subject and *'went to school'* is the predicate.

Prefix: a prefix is a morpheme which can be added to the beginning of a word to change its meaning.

Preposition: a preposition is a word like *at, over, by* and *with*. It is usually followed by a noun phrase.

Semantics: the study of the meanings of words.

Suffix: a suffix is a morpheme which is added to the end of a word.

Synonym: words which have the same meaning as another word, or very similar: *wet/damp*.

Syntax: the study of sentence structure, i.e. how words are used together in a sentence.

Verb: a verb is a word that expresses an action, a happening, a process or a state. It can be thought of as a 'doing' or 'being' word.

Exam board specifications

Literature

Topic	AQA A	AQA B	OCR	EdEcxel
Shakespeare	Coursework or examination	Coursework: emphasis on context and performance	Examination: emphasis on context	Examination or coursework: emphasis on context
Poetry	Open book examination pre-1900 or contemporary	Examination pre-1900	Open text examination	Open text examination
Prose	Examination post 1900	Open text examination pre or post 1900	Open text examination pre or post 1900	Examination pre 1900
Drama	Open text examination	Examination pre-1900	not specified: coursework	Open text examination

Language

Topic	AQA A	AQA B	OCR	EdEcxel
Systematic framework for language Study:	**Discovering language -** influences on language use:	**Introduction to the study of language** (including spoken language):	**Description of English -** structural system of language:	**Textual commentary -** structure and meaning, conventions of spoken and written language:
Examination	Examination	Examination	Examination	Examination
Original writing/presentation of texts	**Using language -** analysis and presentation of texts:	**Original writing -** creating texts for different audiences/purposes:	**Experiments in writing -** create, recreate and adapt writing:	**Desk study -** create, recreate and adapt writing:
	Coursework or exam	Coursework	Coursework	Examination
Spoken language	**Interacting through language -** concepts and issues in spoken language:			Textual commentary (included in):
	Examination			Examination
Language in context		**Language and social context -** occupational groups, gender and power:	**Language variation -** speech and accent, child language acquisition, historical features:	**Language of the media:**
		Examination	Examination	Exam or coursework

Language and Literature

Topic	AQA A	AQA B	OCR	EdEcxel
Two literary genres	**Poetry** - emphasis on context and structural frameworks: Examination	**The changing face of literature** - pairs of texts linked by theme, showing language change over time: Examination	**Poetry and prose** - close textual comment: Examination	**Shorter fiction study** - short stories: Coursework or exam
Analysis of literary and non-literary texts, including speech	**The language of prose and speech:** Examination	**Introduction to the study of language and literature** - a range of texts in a small anthology based on Wilfred Owen: Examination	**Linking language and literature** - linguistic and literary features of a range of texts: Examination	**The spoken word** - including analysis of literary drama: Examination
Original writing and production of texts	**Language production** - comment, recreation and adaptation of texts: Coursework	**Production of texts** - different audiences and purposes: Coursework	**Styles of writing:** Coursework	**Desk study** - comment, recreation and adaptation of texts: Coursework

AS Guru™ English

Acknowledgements

Every effort has been made to trace the copyright holders of the material used in this book. If, however, any omissions have been made, we would be happy to rectify this. Please contact us at the address on the title page.

p. 3   Key Skills information taken from www.qca.org.uk web site.

p. 12   Guterson, David, *Snow Falling on Cedars*, published by Bloomsbury Books, 1995.

p. 23   Tremain, Rose, *Music and Silence*, published by Chatto & Windus, 1999, reprinted by permission of Sheil Land Associates Ltd.

p. 23   Greene, Graham, *Brighton Rock*, published by Bodley Head, Random House Group Limited, 1970.

p. 24   Marquez, Gabriel Garcia, *Chronicle of a Death Foretold*, published by Jonathan Cape, 1982, reprinted by permission of Random House Group Limited.

p. 24   Extract from *Midnight's Children* by Salman Rushdie, published by Jonathan Cape. Used by permission of the Random House Group Limited.

p. 26   Rubin, Harriet, *The Princessa: Machiavelli for Women,* published by Bloomsbury Books, 1987.

p. 26   Chick, Sandra, 'Don't Look Back' from *Factor 25: A Collection of Steamy Summer Love Stories,* published by Livewire, Women's Press Ltd, 1999, copyright held by the author.

p. 42   Gunn, Thom, 'Tamer and Hawk', *Selected Poems 1950–1975*, reprinted by permission of Faber and Faber Ltd.

p. 47   Atwood, Margaret, 'Half-hanged Mary', *Morning in the Burned House*, published by Virago Poetry, 1995.

p. 47   Jennings, Elizabeth, 'Rembrandt's Self-portraits', *Collected Poems*, published by Carcanet, 1986.

p. 48   Nichols, Grace, 'Alone', *Fat Black Woman's Poems,* published by Virago, reprinted by permission of Little Brown.

p. 51   Ferlinghetti, Lawrence, 'Short Story on a Painting of Gustav Klimt', *These are My Rivers: New and Selected Poems 1955–1993*, published by New Directions, 1994.

p. 54   Armitage, Simon, 'Very Simply Topping Up the Brake Fluid' taken from *Zoom* published by Bloodaxe Books.

p. 64   Williams, Tennessee, *A Streetcar named Desire,* Penguin Plays, Methuen Publishing Ltd, 1984.

p. 65, 73   Ibsen, Hendrik, *A Doll's House* Methuen Student Edition, Methuen Publishing Ltd, 1985.

p. 86   Train Company train ticket.

p. 86   Chocolate and Vanilla Ice-Cream Croissants recipe from *Real Food* by Nigel Slater, Fourth Estate, 1997.

p. 87   Anti-drugs poster, National Drugs Helpline, Department of Health. Crown copyright material is reproduced with the permission of the Controller of Her Majesty's Stationary Office.

p. 87   Music ticket, reprinted with permission of BBC Radio 1.

p. 87   Cover of British Gas leaflet. With the permission of British Gas Trading Limited.

p. 93   'Why am I jealous?' from *AQA English Language Specimen Units and Mark Schemes, Spec. A.*

p. 94   Lawrence, D.H., *Sons and Lovers,* published by Penguin Books Ltd, 1995.

p. 94   Atwood, Margaret, *The Handmaid's Tale*, published by Vintage Books, 1996.

p. 96-97   From a letter by T.S. Eliot to his six year-old niece, Theodora, from *The Letters of T S Eliot,* edited by Valerie Eliot, extracts dated 1911

p. 89, 100   Crystal, David, *Cambridge Encyclopedia of Lanugage*, published by Cambridge University Press, 1995.

p. 101   International Phonetic Alphabet from *Living Language* by Keith & Shuttleworth, published by Hodder & Stoughton, 1987.

p. 102   'Where School is a Bowl of Cherries' from the *Guardian* Education, Tuesday July 11 2000.

p. 102   London Today interview with Dan Keech from Common Ground, Carlton TV, broadcast 18 July 2000.

p. 105   Words of Passage diagram, taken from 'Roots to the Future, Ethnic Diversity in the Making of Britain' reprinted by permission of the Commission for Racial Equality.

p. 110   Page from the Playlouder.com web site, printed with the kind permission of Playlouder.com.

p. 112   An Introduction by Geri Halliwell, *6BillionandOne*, United Nations.

Further reading

Below is a list of some books you could read to find out more about critical theories (see page 31). They are not essential reading for your AS English course, but are useful if you are interested in literary criticism and want to expand your knowledge of the subject.

• *The Art of Fiction* by David Lodge (Penguin). This is a great introduction to the craft of the fiction writer. It contains good examples of extracts to illustrate the terms.

• *Literary Terms: A Practical Glossary* (Chalkface Press, published in Britain by The English and Media Centre, 18 Compton Terrace, London N1 2UN). This book guides the reader trhrough a series of exercises to an understanding of literary theory.

If you are planning to go on to study at A2 or even University level, this book could be very useful to you

• *Fifty Key Contemporary Thinkers – From Structuralism to Postmodernity* by John Lechte (Routledge, an imprint of Taylor and Francis Books Ltd.). This book surveys the most important figures who have influenced post-War thought, and provides a link between the Arts and Social Sciences.